EARLY CHILDHOOD EDUCATION SERIES

Leslie R. Williams, Editor   Millie Almy, Senior Advisor

(Continued)

WIDENING THE CIRCLE

Including Children with Disabilities
in Preschool Programs

Edited by Samuel L. Odom

*with Paula J. Beckman, Marci J. Hanson, Eva Horn,
Joan Lieber, Susan R. Sandall, Ilene S. Schwartz, and
Ruth A. Wolery*

FOREWORD BY CAROL COPPLE

Teachers College, Columbia University
New York and London

Published by Teachers College Press, 1234 Amsterdam Avenue, New York, NY 10027

Library of Congress Cataloging-in-Publication Data

Widening the circle: including children with disabilities in preschool programs/edited by Samuel L. Odom; with Paula J. Beckman ... [et al.]; foreword by Carol Copple.
    p.   cm. — (Early childhood education series)
    Includes bibliographical references and index.
    ISBN 0-8077-4172-8 (cloth: alk. paper) — ISBN 0-8077-4171-X (pbk.: alk. paper)
    1. Handicapped children—Education (Preschool)—United States. 2. Education, Preschool—United States. I. Odom, Samuel L. II. Beckman, Paula J., 1952- III. Early childhood education series (Teachers College Press)

LC4019.2 .C36 2001
371.9′0472—dc21   2001041576

ISBN 0-8077-4171-X (paper)
ISBN 0-8077-4172-8 (cloth)

Printed on acid-free paper
Manufactured in the United States of America

09 08 07 06 05 04 03 02   8 7 6 5 4 3 2 1

Contents

Foreword

IN A TRULY SEISMIC SHIFT from 1988 to the present, preschool children with disabilities have entered inclusive classes in unprecedented numbers. Yet the movement to inclusive classes has been largely from resource room; the proportion of children served in self-contained classes actually has remained roughly the same at about 50%. Despite the dramatic move to inclusion, there are a great many children with disabilities that it has not reached. Even when children are in programs that might be called inclusive, many of them experience inclusion to only a limited extent. The authors of this volume are tackling a critical question: What facilitates or impedes preschool inclusion?

Looking at administrators' and teachers' attitudes and practices could shed light on preschool inclusion. Varying social policies, too, may make a difference. Or perhaps researchers should look at what families want most for their children. Which of these factors makes a difference in determining when and how preschool inclusion takes place? The answer, of course, is "all of the above." To understand and improve preschool inclusion requires a well-developed picture of *all* these facets, and others as well, and how they interact.

The contributors to WIDENING THE CIRCLE know this. Taking an ecological approach to studying preschool inclusion, they examine interacting spheres that shape and influence it, including classroom environment, peer interaction, families, communities, cultural and linguistic diversity, and social policy.

Odom and his colleagues also recognize that preschool inclusion cannot be understood simply by examining the substantial literature on K–12 inclusion. The world of early care and education differs dramatically from that of elementary and secondary schools. Not only do young children relate differently than do older children, but teachers and administrators also operate under very different conditions. All of this takes place within a patchwork landscape sharply distinct from that of the schools.

Clearly, insight into how preschool inclusion fares must be sought in early childhood settings, and in a considerable a range of settings at that—extensive enough to reflect the widely varying contexts of early care and education. And a question of such complexity calls for investigators who understand that one-dimensional answers are bound to be wrong.

The work reported here comes from a 5-year national research project based at five universities in different parts of the country. Although WIDENING THE CIRCLE looks like an edited volume, it is the product of something far rarer in the world of research: a true collaboration. In the Early Childhood Research Institute on Inclusion (ECRII), each researcher's perspective and focus are clearly enriched by the others' work and thinking. Sam Odom serves as lead editor, with major contributions from the seven other ECRII investigators, all highly respected early childhood special educators and researchers in their own right.

These are not ivory tower researchers. Odom, Beckman, Hanson, Horn, Lieber, Sandall, Schwartz, and Wolery have abundant direct experience with inclusion in all its forms and facets. They have spent a great deal of time in early childhood programs and with the children and families they write about here. WIDENING THE CIRCLE shows the enormous benefits of collaborative work at ground zero.

As an early childhood educator I am reminded by this book that early childhood and special education have considerable compatibility of philosophy and approach. There are differences, to be sure, but here the similarities stand out. Both fields strongly emphasize children's social, emotional, and physical development as well as their cognitive development and learning. Both special education and early childhood professionals pay close attention to what is individually effective and developmentally appropriate. Far more than other educators, they see parents as full partners in promoting children's learning and well being. And importantly, they recognize that children's lives in and out of the program are highly relevant to curriculum goals and content.

At the same time, this book also shows how much we in early childhood education can learn from special education. In the research and implications for practice described, early childhood practitioners will find much that is useful. For example, there is solid information and helpful suggestions for modifying activities, materials, environmental supports, and teaching strategies for individual children; communicating and collaborating with parents; and building in individualized learning opportunities throughout the preschool day.

A closer look at this last point illustrates the usefulness of special educators' perspectives and knowledge for early childhood practitioners. According to Eva Horn and her colleagues (Chapter 4), the premise behind embedded learning opportunities is that "although many early childhood programs offer learning opportunities across the day, children with disabilities may need guidance and support in order to recognize and learn from these opportunities." The same is true of many if not all children in a given early childhood program. A child learning English or a child from a home with no books, for example, also needs individualized guidance and support to achieve key learning goals. For these children too, teachers will do well to plan embedded learning opportunities to occur regularly within certain activities and routines. Many teachers already do, but many do not. The authors' suggestions regarding embedded learning opportunities should help early childhood teachers to think about and provide individualized learning experiences on a regular basis.

Of the many points of interest I found in this book, I will mention one more. Odom and his colleagues make clear that inclusion, as well as quality, looks different in different preschool programs and means different things to different people. They provide a set of quality indicators in Chapter 2, but they emphasize that it is not intended as a list of dos and don'ts for programs. Rather, it is a tool to use to talk together.

We can all learn from this balanced, nonprescriptive attitude toward making use of expert knowledge to inform practice. It recognizes both sides of the coin—that the knowledge base should be used to enhance practice, but not to the exclusion of what frontline practitioners know and do. As useful as research-based quality indicators (or guidelines for developmentally appropriate practice, for that matter) may be, they offer only a starting point for ongoing conversations about improving programs for children. Throughout WIDENING THE CIRCLE one finds this refreshing outlook: a commitment to increasing the knowledge and understanding of preschool inclusion, but without any undertone of "We're the experts and we know best" when it comes to connecting with families, practitioners, and communities.

Carol Copple
*National Association for the
Education of Young Children*

Acknowledgments

AS RESEARCHERS, WE ARE VERY GRATEFUL for the support, assistance, and collaboration extended to us by the many individuals involved in this work. Our research began with 16 inclusive programs located in the San Francisco Bay Area, the College Park and Baltimore areas of Maryland, the middle Tennessee and Louisville, Kentucky, areas, and the Seattle and Vancouver areas of Washington. It extended to the Chapel Hill, North Carolina, area during the third year of the project and to Indiana in the fifth year. To ensure anonymity, we cannot name the individual programs, but we want to thank the administrators who first allowed us into their programs, the teachers who allowed us into their classrooms, the family members who talked to us for hours on end, and in some cases, over several years, and the children who allowed us to follow them around the classroom and observe their every move.

In addition to the co-authors of the chapters in this book, other individuals have been our colleagues and co-investigators on the project. They include Beth Brennan, Bill Brown, Susan Janko, Ann Kaiser, Jules Marquart, Cap Peck, and Pamela Wolfberg. They began the project with us or joined us along the way, and contributed to our program of research. We can add to this list David Fetterman, who was our methodological consultant, qualitative research guide, and manic empowerment guru during the early, crucial stages of our project. Christine Hikado and Jay Chambers at the Center for Special Education Finance at the American Institutes for Research contributed the expertise in conducting our cost analyses.

We were very lucky to have recruited a wise and experienced advisory board that provided great assistance at crucial times during the project. The advisory board members were Diane Bricker, Wes Brown, Michael Conn-Powers, Linda Espinosa, Diane Fergusan, Beth Harry, Mark Innocenti, Irving Lazar, Mary McEvoy, Margaret McLaughlin, Sandra Panyan, Theresa Rebhorn, Diane Sainato, and Chris Salisbury, and we thank them.

At all our sites, we have been very fortunate to have had talented and superlative master's, doctoral, and postdoctoral students who partici-

pated in our project. These included, from Vanderbilt University, Leslie
Craig-Unkefer, Bill Frea, Marny Helfrich, Ariane Holcombe, Laura How-
ard, Jennifer Hurley, Martha Katz, Patti McKenna, Pam Pallis, Amy Solo-
mon-Harris, and Denise Williams; from San Francisco State University,
Sonja Gutierrez Mathias and Craig Zercher; from the University of Maryland, Deirdre Barnwell, Irene Brodsky, Karen Capell, Beth Caron, Moni-
malika Day, Krista Kettler, Amy Kappel, Heide Lee, Helen Sherry, Marci
Spiotta, Jennifer Stepanek, Shana Thompson, Jennifer Tschantz, Tracy
Wayne, and Kerry Wolfe; from the University of Washington, Kris Anderson, Hsin-Ying Chou, Carolyn Cottam, Ann Garfinkle, Gail Joseph, and
Karly Lewallen; from the University of North Carolina, YoungShul Choi,
Elaine Cusick, Dianne Gut, Susan McClanahan, and Margaret Sigalove;
and from Indiana University, Ling-Ling Tsao.

At the University of Washington, Jennifer Annable, the principal of
the Experimental Education Unit, was extremely helpful in providing
feedback and advice. Two outstanding administrative assistants, Dolly
Geragano and Kriste Kuczynski, aided the organization of the project.
Last but certainly not least, our two project officers, Gail Houle from the
Office of Special Education Programs and Naomi Karp from the Office
of Educational Research and Improvement, provided both the funds and
the organizational support that allowed the project to operate.

CHAPTER 1

Learning About the Barriers to and Facilitators of Inclusion for Young Children with Disabilities

Samuel L. Odom

KELLY WAS 4 YEARS OLD when we first met her. She was a spunky, talkative bundle of energy, standing 3½ feet tall with dark brown hair. She had been blind from birth. She and her family had participated in the early intervention program in her rural southern community when Kelly was younger, and when she turned 3, Kelly enrolled in a public school special education class containing children with other disabilities. Claire, Kelly's mother, was not entirely pleased with that option because Kelly's class "had too many severely handicapped children. Kelly was the only one in the class that could talk" (parent interview). Claire was glad when, the next year, the local school system and the local Head Start program organized a class in which there would be children from Head Start and children with disabilities. In this new class, there was a Head Start teacher and a special education teacher, as well as two assistants. Claire and her family continued to look at other options for Kelly, ones that would meet her special needs. Claire told us about visiting the "School of the Blind" in the state and why they decided on the inclusive program instead for Kelly.

> We, my mom [Kelly's grandmother] and me, went to the blind school for a summer preschool conference. I just don't think it is the place for Kelly. They have rails all down the hallways. Everywhere you go there is braille, braille, braille. . . . I like it [Kelly's inclusive preschool] because she's going to school with, well, normal kids. . . . She's got a lot of interaction with kids that there's nothing wrong with them. . . . She needs to learn how to get around and get along with people who can see and how to act and how to take care of herself and behave herself in public like she should. . . . That's the biggest thing. (parent interview)

For Kelly's family, it was important for Kelly to become a member of this class in which there were typical children her age doing typical things. They felt that by becoming a member of this class, Kelly was taking an important step toward becoming a member of the world.

In this book, we tell the story of our research on preschool inclusion, in which Kelly, her family, and her teachers were among the participants.

We are a group of researchers who originally were located at four universities. In 1994, the federal government funded us, through a 5-year project called the Early Childhood Research Institute on Inclusion (ECRII). After a year's no-cost extension, the ECRII project ended in August 2000. The first purpose of our research was to learn about how inclusive preschool programs work, what factors influence their success (which we call facilitators), and what factors stand in the way of success (which we call barriers). The second purpose of our research was to use this information to create teaching strategies and ways of working with teachers, other professionals, family members, and administrators in order to support the successful inclusion of young children with disabilities in programs with typically developing children—that is, to help young children become members of the class as one step toward becoming members of the world in which they live.

In this chapter, I begin the story of our research project. I explain how inclusion at the preschool level has come about and how it is different from inclusion in elementary, middle, and high schools. The conceptual framework for our research is briefly described, followed by an overview of the book. What we have learned about preschool inclusion unfolds in subsequent chapters.

WHAT IS PRESCHOOL INCLUSION?

A question that we and others have asked is, "What is preschool inclusion?" In our research, we were interested in having the participants—children (through their behavior), teachers and other professionals, family members, administrators—tell us their meaning of inclusion, rather than having us as researchers bring a strict definition from our academic ivory towers. However, we had to start somewhere, so we initially defined inclusion very broadly as classroom programs in which children with and without disabilities participate. We discuss the perspectives of participants in Chapter 2 and also draw overall conclusions about definitions in the synthesis points we have identified in Chapter 11.

At the outset, it is very important to note that inclusion extends far beyond the classroom setting. The funding for our research limited most of our work to classroom- and program-based issues (but see Chapter 8 on community issues). However, inclusion also refers to participation in the broad range of activities that normally occur for typically developing children in their community and culture. The research of our colleagues Carl Dunst, Mary Beth Bruder, Carol Trivette, and others has made great headway in understanding the natural learning opportunities that occur in homes and community (Dunst, Hamby, Trivette, Raab, & Bruder, in press). We believe that inclusion at the preschool level is one, but not the only, important context in which children prepare for becoming members of the world.

How Did Preschool Inclusion Develop?

One can trace the roots of modern preschool inclusion programs to the university-based programs begun in the 1970s by Diane and William Bricker (Bricker, 2000; Bricker & Bricker, 1971) and Eileen Allen (Allen, Benning, & Drummond, 1972). Another early impetus was through Head Start, which in the 1970s was the first large-scale national program to actively include children with disabilities. The first national public school initiative for preschool inclusion began with the original Education for the Handicapped Act (PL 94-142) in 1975, which contained a provision that children with disabilities be educated in the least restrictive environment (LRE). This act allowed states, if they chose, to use federal funds for services for preschool children with disabilities. A decade later, the Individuals with Disabilities Education Act (PL 99-457, IDEA) created a mandate that states provide services for preschool children with disabilities by 1991 and maintained the LRE provision. Subsequent reauthorizations of IDEA have strengthened the LRE provision as well as specified that, at least for infants and toddlers, services be provided in "natural environments"(PL 105-17).

Beginning with the original law in 1975, and continuing to the present, preschool children receiving services from school systems must have an Individualized Education Plan (IEP). This plan is developed, ideally, by a team of professionals (a special education teacher, speech pathologist, principal or other administrator, and, hopefully, early childhood education teacher—if the child is in an inclusive setting). The parents or other family members also should be important participants on this team. Together the team establishes the educational goals for the child and individual objectives for meeting those goals. The team then makes a decision about placement, usually in a class setting, that will best lead to the child accomplishing his or her educational goals. The most recent revision of the law (PL 105-17) requires that inclusive program placements be considered first, and that only if a child's learning needs are not able to be met in the inclusive setting, should placement in a nonintegrated setting be considered.

These laws have had an impact on the numbers of preschool children with disabilities receiving services and the locations of such services. The latest government statistics indicate that from 1988 to 1997, the total number of preschool children receiving services has increased 168% (U.S. Department of Education, 1999). Also, across the years, there has been a steady rise in the percentage of preschool children with disabilities enrolled in inclusive classes (from 40% in 1987–88 to 50% in 1996–97). However, as Don Bailey (2000) has pointed out, the increased percentages have come from children moving from resource rooms to inclusive settings, and there has not been a major decrease in children enrolled in self-contained classes. In 1997, about 50% of the children with disabilities receiving services were in inclusive settings. For the other 50%, it appears that there are still barriers to placement in early childhood settings with typically developing children.

What Makes Inclusion at the Preschool Level Unique?

If you were going to try to break down the barriers to preschool inclusion, you might think that looking at the research on inclusion and mainstreaming for older students would be useful, and it is in some cases (e.g., the literature on collaboration). However, we and others have found that inclusion at the preschool level is markedly different from inclusion in elementary, middle, and high schools (Odom et al., 2001); for example:

- In many public schools, there are no preschool classes for normally developing children. As a result, administrators and parents have to look outside public school buildings (i.e., in Head Start or community-based programs) to find possible inclusive settings for preschool children with disabilities, and in looking for these inclusive opportunities, they sometimes run into substantial barriers.
- The nature of the curriculum is different in early childhood programs and in elementary–middle–high school programs. Early childhood programs take a more "developmentally appropriate" approach to curriculum planning (Bredekamp & Copple, 1997), while general education programs for older children are more academically oriented.
- The developmental skills of young children differ from those of older children. For preschool children, there may be less developmental difference between children with disabilities and their same-aged peers than occurs in classes for older children. Also, social relationships with peers appear to be less firmly fixed for young children than for older children.
- The pressures of "high-stakes" achievement testing have not extended down to the preschool level. For older children, the impact of achievement testing has had implications for curriculum plan-

ning (i.e., curriculum may be directed more narrowly toward the form and content of the achievement tests) and inclusion (i.e., reluctance to include children with disabilities in classes because their achievement test scores will bring down the class average).

Although some common issues exist, these points highlight the differences between inclusion for preschool and school-aged children. At the preschool level, there are unique features of programs and communities that create successful inclusive opportunities for young children with disabilities, but there are also unique barriers.

OUR CONCEPTUAL FRAMEWORK

Because our work involved many researchers located in different parts of the country, it was especially important that we began with, and used throughout our studies, a common theoretical framework. We all believed that barriers to and facilitators of inclusive programs were located within classrooms (e.g., accessibility to activities and materials, use of specialized instruction), but we also thought there might be factors operating outside the classroom setting that had a powerful influence on inclusion. In addition, we all strongly held the value that family members' perspectives should be an essential part of any research on preschool inclusion.

The ecological systems theory of development proposed by Urie Bronfenbrenner (1979; Bronfenbrenner & Morris, 1998) was an ideal conceptual model for our research. In this model, a child is thought to participate in different settings or contexts (called *microsystems* by Bronfenbrenner). A microsystem could be a preschool classroom, the home, Sunday school, or a neighborhood play group. For much of our research, we focused on the inclusive preschool classroom or program as the context for inclusion (as highlighted in Figure 1.1). We assumed that there were features of those settings that influenced the way they operated and the experiences of children. However, other things affected the inclusive classroom setting as well.

It is also possible that events happening in one microsystem context might influence events in another microsystem context. Bronfenbrenner called these *mesosystem* influences. For example, if a child and parent had an argument at home, the child might remain angry when at school, with the anger spilling over into his or her play with peers. On a more positive note, the teacher at a child's school may write a note home to the parents describing the new words the child has been learning at school, and the parents may start to use the words in their conversations with the child at home.

Influence on microsystems also might be exerted by individuals who have never been in or seen the microsystem. These are called *exosystem* influences. For example, we suspected that social policies at the local, state, or national level would influence the ways that preschool classrooms operated. These policies usually are established by people who never or rarely enter classrooms. The federal laws described previously represent an exosystem influence.

Last, there also might be influences at the societal level or related to the culture of the family that affect preschool classrooms. Bronfenbrenner called these *macrosystem* influences. For example, the societal attitude of accepting individuals with disabilities as members of the community has been reflected in more open enrollment policies for children with disabilities in child care settings.

It is also possible for influences from these different contexts to have reciprocal effects—that is, the influence is not always from the top (exosystem or macrosystem) down (to the mesosystem or microsystem). For example, social policy factors could affect the curriculum in classroom settings, but teachers' experiences with using a curriculum in the classroom could provide feedback that might affect social policies.

We used Bronfenbrenner's ecological systems framework to plan our large-scale study of inclusive preschool programs operating in four regional locations in the United States. This study, conducted during the first 2 years of our project, became the foundation for the rest of our research. In Appendix A we provide details about the settings and participants in our study, the methods followed in collecting our research data, and the general mode of analysis for many of the findings that have come out of this study. The specific findings are described in subsequent chapters. Our general guiding question was: What are the barriers to and facilitators of preschool inclusion?

HOW THIS BOOK
IS ORGANIZED

Chapter 2 describes the ways in which individuals define inclusion. The organization of the remainder of the book follows Bronfenbrenner's ecological systems conceptual framework. Focusing first on the microsystem—the classroom—we describe, in Chapters 3, 4, and 5, the ways children participate in classrooms, how teachers promote children's learning, and how children develop social relationships with peers. Widening our gaze to encompass the mesosystem, Chapters 6, 7, and 8 examine how teachers and other professionals collaborate with one another and family members, how families think about inclusion, and how children and families participate in the community. Chapter 9 looks at how social policy affects inclusion—the exosystem influence. The macrosystem influences are taken up in Chapter 10, which examines the effects of cultural and linguistic diversity. In each of these chapters, we conclude with the implications for children, teachers, families, administrators, and others who are part of the inclusion process. The book concludes with a discussion, in Chapter 11, of synthesis points that summarize the overall findings supported by our research.

REFERENCES

Allen, K. E., Benning, P. M., & Drummond, W. T. (1972). Integration of normal and handicapped children in a behavior modification preschool: A case study. In G. Semb (Ed.), *Behavior analysis and education* (pp. 127–141). Lawrence: University of Kansas Press.

Bailey, D. B. (2000, August). *Issues and perspectives on inclusion.* Keynote presentation at NECTAS Conference on Children, Families, and Inclusive Communities, Chapel Hill, NC.

Bredekamp, S., & Copple, C. (Eds.). (1997). *Developmentally appropriate practice in early childhood programs* (rev. ed.). Washington, DC: National Association for the Education of Young Children.

Bricker, D. (2000). Inclusion: How the scene has changed. *Topics in Early Childhood Special Education, 20,* 14–20.

Bricker, D., & Bricker, W. (1971). *Toddler Research and Intervention Project Report— Year 1.* (IMRID Behavioral Science Monograph No. 20). Nashville, TN: Institute on Mental Retardation and Intellectual Development.

Bronfenbrenner, U. (1979). *The ecology of human development: Experiments by nature and design.* Cambridge, MA: Harvard University Press.

Bronfenbrenner, U., & Morris, P. A. (1998). The ecology of developmental process. In R. Lerner (Ed.), *Handbook of child psychology: Vol. 1. Theoretical models of human development* (5th ed.; pp. 993–1028). New York: Wiley.

Dunst, C. J., Hamby, D., Trivette, C. M., Raab, M., & Bruder, M. B. (in press). Sources of naturally occurring children's learning opportunities in the context of family and community life. *Journal of Early Intervention.*

Fogel, A., & Melson, J. F. (1988). *Child development.* St. Paul, MN: West.

Odom, S. L., Wolery, R., Lieber, J., Sandall, S., Hanson, M. J., Beckman, P. J., Schwartz, I., & Horn, E. (2001). *Preschool inclusion: A review of research from an ecological systems perspective.* Manuscript submitted for publication.

U.S. Department of Education. (1999). *To assure the free appropriate public education of all children with disabilities: Twenty-first annual report to Congress on the implementation of the Individuals with Disabilities Education Act.* Washington, DC: Author.

CHAPTER 2

"I Know It When I See It": In Search of a Common Definition of Inclusion

Ilene S. Schwartz, Susan R. Sandall, Samuel L. Odom, Eva Horn, & Paula J. Beckman

RACHEL, LEV, AND AMANDA ARE 4-year-old children with Down syndrome. They all live in the same metropolitan area and attend inclusive early childhood programs. Here is where the similarities end. Although all three of the early childhood programs they attend identify themselves as inclusive, the ways in which inclusion is described, implemented, and supported are different. The differences in inclusive practices across these three programs are not minor issues of description, nor are they merely the normal differences we expect to see across high-quality early childhood programs. The programs differ on such major dimensions as who can attend the program, how children with special needs receive necessary support and specialized instruction, staff training, and the amount of time children with and without disabilities spend in the same classroom.

This lack of clarity and consistency regarding a common definition of inclusion is not unique to these three early childhood programs. As part of the research we conducted with the Early Childhood Research Institute on Inclusion, we found that how inclusion was defined varied across researchers, practitioners, family members, advocates, school administrators, and consumers of inclusive programs. Not only is there no commonly accepted definition of inclusion, there is little consensus about whether there are key elements that must be present before a program can be called "inclusive." Inclusion, like education in general, will always be under the influence of local control, beliefs, and standards; but having an agreed-on basic definition is important as we attempt to conduct research, train staff, and work with parents to create programs that meet their needs and those of their children.

The purpose of this chapter is to propose a list of key characteristics of inclusive programs. Using this list as our starting point, we will compare and contrast the different inclusive experiences provided to the three children—Rachel, Lev, and Amanda—introduced earlier. Finally, we will present a list of guiding questions that educational teams and families can use to begin their discussions about planning and improving their own inclusive programs.

KEY CHARACTERISTICS OF INCLUSIVE
EARLY CHILDHOOD PROGRAMS

As noted in Chapter 1, one of the goals of the ECRII was to identify barriers to and facilitators of inclusion in early childhood programs. Before we could begin our search for practices and policies that were standing in the way of inclusion or greasing its wheels, we needed to come to a common understanding of what our research team meant by the term *inclusion*. This task was far more difficult than any of us had anticipated. One reason for this difficulty was that we all brought our own preconceptions about inclusion to the table. These impressions, opinions, and biases were formed by years of teaching, conducting research, working with families, and reading the professional literature. What was surprising to all of us was the diversity of our opinions about a definition that each of us thought was fairly straightforward. To help set the context for our discussions, we present three common definitions of inclusion from the professional literature. These definitions come from a textbook used in undergraduate early childhood education classes (Allen & Schwartz, 2001), a position statement from a professional organization (Division for Early Childhood, 2000), and a professional book specifically about inclusion (Stainback & Stainback, 1990):

Inclusion is not a set of strategies or a placement issue. Inclusion is about belonging to a community—a group of friends, a school community, or a neighborhood. (Allen & Schwartz, 2001, p. 2)

Inclusion as a value supports the right of all children regardless of their diverse abilities to participate actively in natural settings within their communities. A natural setting is one in which the child would spend time if he or she had not had a disability. Such settings include, but are not limited to home and family play groups, child care, nursery school, Head Start programs, kindergartens, and neighborhood school classrooms. (DEC, 2000)

Inclusion means providing all students within the mainstream appropriate educational programs that are challenging yet geared to their capabilities and needs as well as any support and assistance they and/or their teachers may need to be successful in the mainstream. But an inclusive school also goes beyond this. An inclusive school is a place where everyone belongs, is accepted, supports, and is supported by her or her peers and other members of the school community in the course of having his or her educational needs met. (Stainback & Stainback, 1990, p. 3)

What is interesting about all three of these definitions is the lack of specificity they provide. All of the definitions provide readers with a starting point to discuss the philosophy of inclusion, but none address any specifics of implementation. In our own attempts to define inclusion, we quickly realized that "the devil is in the details." We could all agree with the definitions stated previously, but as we began to look closely at community programs that called themselves inclusive, we could not all agree on whether these programs crossed that invisible line that made them inclusive. For each of us, the line separating inclusive programs from noninclusive programs was in a different place. Some of the difficult questions we pondered included the following:

- At what ratio should an inclusive program include children with and without disabilities? Could a program be considered inclusive if there were more children with disabilities than without? At what ratio does a classroom no longer warrant the label inclusive?
- Do the children with and without disabilities need to be enrolled in the same classroom for a program to be called inclusive? Can they be enrolled in neighboring classrooms that come together for some activities? If so, how much time do the children need to spend together for the program to be considered inclusive?
- If children with and without disabilities are enrolled in the same classroom, is it an inclusive program if the children with disabilities have a different schedule (e.g., more hours or fewer hours) than the typically developing children? If so, how much time do the children need to spend together for the program to be considered inclusive?
- Can inclusive classrooms have entry criteria for both the children with and those without disabilities, or should any child who lives in the community and meets the age requirements of the program be enrolled? In other words, is inclusion for everyone?
- What types of specialized instruction and support must be provided to the children with disabilities for the program to be considered inclusive? Is it inclusion when teachers treat all children the same, without making accommodations or modifications for their special needs?

All of these questions were prompted by real situations we encountered during our observations and interviews as we studied 16 "inclusive" early childhood programs across the country. For several reasons, we decided not to attempt to answer these questions directly. These include:

1. Inclusion is a process. As early childhood programs begin to be implemented, some changes will be gradual as new staff are brought on board. High-quality programs change to reflect the strengths, needs, beliefs, and attitudes of participating staff and families.

2. Inclusion, to a great extent, is defined and controlled locally. Regional differences and community standards are important in creating programs that are a good match with the children and families they serve and the educational staff they employ.
3. Just as individualization is a cornerstone of planning appropriate educational programs for children with disabilities, it is also important to consider the individual when defining inclusion. Ultimately an inclusive program must meet the needs of an individual child and family—this criterion must guide researchers and practitioners, reminding us that flexibility may well be an important common characteristic of high-quality inclusive programs.

Instead of creating a specific definition, we developed a list of key characteristics of inclusive programs (see Figure 2.1). The purpose of these key characteristics was not to create a litmus test to determine whether a program was inclusive. In fact, one of the most interesting and surprising things we learned from our research was that a range of programs identified themselves as being "inclusive." Rather, the purpose of the list was to provide our group of researchers a format that we could use to compare and contrast the inclusive programs we studied. Since the programs were so different—which meant that the experiences children and families had were also quite different—we needed a common metric that we could use to make sense of the information we collected about all the programs.

THREE CHILDREN, THREE PROGRAMS, THREE DEFINITIONS OF INCLUSION

To illustrate the differences across inclusive programs, we will compare the programs that Rachel, Lev, and Amanda attended across the key characteristics of inclusive programs. First, however, we will describe briefly each of the programs.

Rachel attended the City Center Child Care (CCCC) program. This program was run by a private nonprofit organization that provided services to people with mental retardation across the life span. The child care program had been in operation for about 20 years and was one of the first inclusive early childhood programs in the city; it still had a reputation for being one of the best.

Lev attended the Building Blocks Head Start program. Located in a church basement in a low-income, ethnically diverse neighborhood, Building Blocks was just a couple of years old.

Amanda attended the Valley View school in Hidden Trails School

Program Philosophy

- Inclusion as a starting point vs. having to earn entrance into an inclusive program
- Value placed on family beliefs, culture, choice, and involvement
- Proportion of children with disabilities to typically developing children in the class

Scheduling

- Enrollment in a class with typical children
- Same schedule (i.e., arrival time and dismissal time) as children without disabilities

Curriculum

- High-quality early childhood program
- A curriculum (defined broadly) that is developmentally appropriate and meets the needs and challenges of all young children in the program
- Support for active participation of children with disabilities in ongoing activities and routines
- Appropriate adaptation and modifications provided
- Instructional needs of children with disabilities met through specialized supports
- Opportunities for peer interactions, with appropriate supports to promote success

Adult Issues

- Support to adults provided by the responsible agencies/systems (e.g., school district, Head Start, child care), including training, release time, appropriate staffing
- Family members involved as active members of the team
- Collaboration of all team members, including families, administrators and ECE/ECSE, and related service professionals

Figure 2.1. Key characteristics of inclusive early childhood programs.

District. This school district was in a rapidly growing suburban area south of the city. Valley View was a sparkling new elementary school, one of two opened by the district the year Amanda started preschool, and it housed an inclusive preschool program as well as a fully inclusive K–5 program.

Program Philosophy

The three programs all identified themselves as being fully inclusive and were recognized in the community as good examples of inclusive programming. How inclusion filtered down into policy and practice, however, looked different in every program. At Rachel's school, CCCC, the philosophy of the program emphasized community as inclusive of children, families, and staff members. The director of this program was purposeful in talking about inclusion being about more than disability. She worked with her staff to build diversity in the program and to foster a sense of belonging among staff, children, and families. For example, about 30% of the children were ethnic minorities, approximately 40% had disabilities, and 30% were from low-income families taking advantage of one of the five different public assistance arrangements that are available. There were three spaces for homeless children in the center, and eight spaces for court-ordered therapeutic child care. The director was also committed to hiring a diverse staff—not just staff from ethnic minorities, but staff who came to CCCC with different life experiences and who personally value and celebrate diversity. As one teacher said:

> We have a very diverse staff here which actually has helped me quite a bit to grow professionally. CCCC encourages diversity within its teaching staff and encourages different opinions and we have an extremely wide range of that here. And for the most part people are very open and accepting. (Teacher H)

Another type of diversity that was obvious among the staff at CCCC is that there were adults with disabilities on the staff who had different types of roles across the school. It was evident that the contributions they made were valued by everyone associated with the school. As the director and teachers said:

> In fact, very soon parents tend to look at their team as being the adult with disabilities and the teachers. . . . During holiday times families typically give gifts to the teaching staff and they never

leave out the aide in the classroom. They always give something to the aide. (Director)

Jim [a classroom aide with disabilities], he's the man. He's our heart and soul. Without Jim, to tell the truth, I don't think there would be a City Center CC. (Teacher D)

We're grateful to have her in the room. She [a classroom aide with disabilities] is a tremendous help. We couldn't make it without her at all. She doesn't have problems with me at all and seems to be like another co-teacher. (Teacher H)

Now let us look at Building Blocks Head Start, which Lev attended. Most visitors were struck by the diversity in the classrooms. Children in the program spoke 11 different languages, and staff spoke 14. When asked who was in their program, one of the head teachers and the program director responded the same way, "We serve the children in our community." Those children had an array of abilities, needs, and concerns. Disability seemed to be just one possible child characteristic; not speaking English was another. The director of the program did have an M.Ed. in special education, but her primary concern was not children with disabilities; her concern was for the children in the community. We remember her description of the enrollment process. Staff, the majority of whom lived in the neighborhood, went door to door to make sure that all eligible children were enrolled. According to the director, eligibility was simple: You had to live in the neighborhood and be 4 years old. Although it was a Head Start program, she never mentioned the economic qualification guidelines. Lev's teacher described her classroom, which included children with disabilities and children who speak many different languages and had their roots in many different countries, by saying lightheartedly, while gesturing to her classroom, "We have a lot of diversity . . . as you see" (Teacher C).

In contrast, at Valley View school, Amanda was not automatically included. As her teacher said, "We went out on a limb to include this child" (Teacher N). Amanda was included only because her mother was a strong advocate who fought for the placement. Amanda's mother told us that she knew it was her right to have her daughter included and that she knew what was best for Amanda. The school district's position was that they offered a continuum of services at preschool and perhaps inclusion was not the best option for Amanda. For example, as the special education director said: "And sometimes it has to do with the abilities of the child. If they're very low functioning, it's the first time they've come into the system, I think they tend to make recommendations for the self-contained classroom because of intensity."

Interestingly, some of the opposition to placing children in inclusive preschool programs came from the teachers who taught the self-contained preschool classrooms. These teachers felt that only the "cream of the crop" got into inclusion and the other children were left for the segregated program. As Amanda's teacher said:

> Another thing is that I've talked to some of the self-contained teachers and a couple of them, there's some jealousy that goes on. And they said, "Well gee, you're taking away our role models [higher functioning children with disabilities], in our classes." But I say, well, my feeling on that is you need to look at it from the standpoint of those kids. Those are the kids that are probably going to exit special ed. and so, I think we owe it to them to let them have the opportunity to mix with the regular kids who do have the social skills to succeed. (Teacher N)

Scheduling

At Lev's and Amanda's schools, the children with and without disabilities attended school on the same days and for the same length of time. Rachel's days were interrupted by a bus ride. In Rachel's situation the public school district decided that the best way to provide specialized instruction for her was to have her attend a segregated special education classroom 4 days a week for 3 hours each day. Everyday after lunch a special education bus arrived at CCCC to pick her up. As other children settled on their cots for a nap, Rachel went off to preschool. When she returned, she joined the other children in whatever afternoon activity was underway.

Although Lev and Amanda had similar schedules to their typically developing peers in their inclusive classrooms, and Rachel had the same schedule for arrival in the morning and going home in the evening, that was not always the case in other programs. Across the 16 programs we studied, we found many programs had different schedules for children with and without disabilities. In one program children with disabilities attended school 5 days a week, 4 hours a day; in that same program typically developing children left an hour earlier and attended school only 3 days a week. In another large early childhood center, children with and without disabilities were in different classrooms most of the day, but their classrooms merge for 20 minutes a day for the inclusive portion of their program.

Curriculum

There was a great deal of difference in curriculum across programs. At CCCC the director believed strongly that all staff members needed to know how to make necessary accommodations and modifications to help all children succeed. Potential teachers spent time in the classrooms as part of the hiring process. Current staff evaluated how they interacted with the children, including the children with disabilities. As the director told us:

> Our program is NAEYC-accredited. We work with our staff to meet the needs of all children—and we really mean all! During the interview process we give applicants an opportunity to work with children with disabilities. So, when a person is hired, we are operating from the same set of expectations. . . . Their comfort level is such that they're going to be flexible and open enough to adapt whatever they do in the classroom. They don't see the kids with disabilities as being somebody else's responsibility, somebody else's problem. (Director)

This director was clear in her statements to staff and families that all children belong and it is the job of staff to help all children have a positive early childhood experience. When children demonstrated challenging behavior, she said to staff and families, "The behavior is not acceptable, but the child stays." She believed it was her job to help all staff work with all children in a positive manner. As she said, "After a period of time you begin to see them [staff] looking more individually at children and less about what their diagnosis is."

At Building Blocks a primary purpose of the curriculum seemed to be to support children with varying developmental levels in the classroom. There were so many children with different language-learning needs and different socialization needs, that making accommodations for a disability did not appear to be an issue for the staff. Although the teachers spoke English during most of the day, they did talk to the children in their native languages and often would call in staff from the office or from another classroom if their language skills were needed. Since many of the children (and the staff) were recent immigrants to the United States, much of the curriculum was centered on helping children make the transition to English and to American schools. For example, one day we watched the children play "Duck, Duck, Goose," with the teacher leading some of the children step-by-step through a game that seemed very new to them. Another day as we observed lunch, a child asked the name of the food being served. The teacher had to refer to the printed menu before he could tell the child that what they were eating for lunch was called "ravioli." One of the teachers described some of these curricular issues from his perspective; interestingly the issue of disability did not come up: "In the first year if they can speak both languages, English and their language, it's better for them. . . . I try to speak Vietnamese as much as I can. . . . I think it's very, very good for the kids to adjust to a new school." He continued, "Here we prepare them how to adjust to a new culture. . . . You see in this classroom we don't do exactly like American classroom. We do something mixed . . . we lead them to a new culture."

At Valley View school the issue of disability was front and center in discussions about curriculum. Teachers had a very clear sense of what was appropriate behavior in the classroom and what was expected from all preschool children. Often when children did not meet those expectations, teachers explained their failure by referring to either the child's disability or unrealistic expectations of parents. For example, Amanda's teacher told us: "She has the capability, I feel, to have friends. She just doesn't want to. . . . There is not enough time in the world to provide the amount of support that Amanda's mother thinks she needs."

The view in the Hidden Trails School District seemed to be that children had to earn their way into inclusion and they could lose their place in that program. Teachers and other support staff attempted to help children be successful, but if they were not successful it was not because of lack of support or inappropriate instruction, but rather due to the child's disability or the behavior the child demonstrated. This attitude had been maintained and, if anything, gotten worse as high-stakes testing in elementary school had been introduced. As the special education director told us:

> There's also pressure from some of those families [families of typi-
> cally developing children] when we had an instance this year with
> some acting out behaviors, screaming, hitting people. The child
> was ultimately moved to another class, but it was really hard for
> the principal and the teacher to say that the classroom could not
> meet the needs of children with disabilities. We don't want your
> child to be at risk, but our commitment here is for these kids [chil-
> dren with disabilities] first.

Adult Issues

At CCCC, perhaps because it was a child care program, families were integral members of the program community. Teachers and parents talked daily during arrival and pick-up times. Clearly, the staff felt responsible for all the children in the program and, to paraphrase a slogan from a disability advocacy group, "All really meant all." For example, a teacher and the director told us:

> So I think basically we have a general responsibility for all the children. And there are certain things that we are working on with Myron or Thad or another child in our class who might be having a problem at that time. (Teacher S)

> And the expectations are that they will adopt, adapt anything they are doing in the classroom for whatever the kid shows they need. (Director)

Although the staff and families at CCCC worked well as a team, relationships with other agencies, especially the local school district, were not as positive and had a negative impact on services for children. For example, as in Rachel's case, most children with disabilities who attended CCCC were removed from their inclusive setting for 3 hours a day for an "educational" placement in a segregated classroom. For whatever reason, the school district and CCCC could not work out a system to provide specialized instruction at the child care program. This lack of cooperation was also evident when it came time to plan children's transitions to kindergarten. Parents, CCCC staff, and school-district staff all stated that this transition planning was often frustrating and stressful. Parents and CCCC staff believed that the school-district officials were too rigid; staff from the school district said that parents and CCCC staff had unrealistic expectations. This lack of teamwork resulted in parents starting off their child's kindergarten year with a negative experience with the school district.

Relations with the public school system were also a problem for the staff at Building Blocks Head Start. The director told us that official "labeling" and identification were a barrier to inclusion in their program because once a child had an IEP, the school system wanted to remove the child from Head Start and place him or her in a segregated classroom. Building Blocks was not a preferred provider of special education services by the school system. As one itinerant teacher who provided services for the school system at Building Blocks told us:

> You know the teachers are good and caring but they are not always trained to do assessment and do the data collection and to deliver services. The kids probably do benefit in some way from

being in the community, but they may not get what we think they would get in a good special education class. (Itinerant Teacher J)

Interestingly, adult issues, such as collaboration and teaming, were the strongest at Hidden Valley. Perhaps it was because it was a school system program, so many of the players at preschool and kindergarten were the same. Once Amanda's mother won her battle to get her daughter into an inclusive setting, the actual planning went very smoothly.

What do we know now about the inclusive experiences of these three children? We know that all three were successfully included (i.e., became members of the class) in their early childhood programs and that the parents of all three were satisfied with the programs. We did not assess the children's developmental skills at the beginning and the end of the year so we do not know whether the specific experiences that occurred under these different definitions of inclusion were related to differences in children's development. We cannot claim that one way of defining inclusion in terms of traditional child outcomes is superior to others.

IMPLICATIONS FOR PRACTICE

Inclusion looks different in different programs. Inclusion means different things to different people. Although these statements seem overly simplistic, they have important implications as we move forward in implementing inclusion more broadly. The "take home" message is that there is no one single "right" way to implement an inclusive program.

It is important to note, however, that we are not saying that there are no quality indicators for inclusive programs. In fact, based on our research and other research in the field (e.g., Guralnick, 2000), we have developed a quality indicator questionnaire that parents and educational teams can use to begin the discussion about inclusive programs (see Figure 2.2). We hope that consumers of programs and program developers will use this tool together to talk about how they perceive the different components of the inclusive classroom. This scale has items that can be rated as low, medium, and high, but users should remember that these ratings are clearly subjective and may vary from observer to observer. Rather than using this scale as a formal quantitative evaluation measure, program providers and consumers are urged to use these questions to guide planning meetings and program improvement plans. Wolery, Pauca, Brashers, and Grant (2000) have developed a systematic and formal assessment of

Guiding Questions	Observer Impression		
Program Philosophy			
1. Do program personnel believe that inclusion is for everyone; that children with and without disabilities benefit?	Low	Medium	High
2. Does the program reflect diverse family beliefs, values, and cultural and linguistic backgrounds?	Low	Medium	High
3. Does the program offer families opportunities for making choices and being involved?	Low	Medium	High
4. Does the program have a shared philosophy across and within responsible systems and agencies?	Low	Medium	High
Program Organization			
1. Is there adequate administrative support and perceived support of program?	Low	Medium	High
2. Are children with disabilities enrolled in a class with typically developing children for the entire day?	Low	Medium	High
3. Do all children have the same opportunities to participate in routines and activities?	Low	Medium	High
4. Are resources allocated in ways that support program philosophies and goals?	Low	Medium	High
5. Is there collaboration of all team members, including families, administrators and ECE/ECSE, and related service professionals across and within systems?	Low	Medium	High
Curriculum			
1. Is the program a high-quality early childhood program?	Low	Medium	High
2. Does the program meet the individual needs of all children?	Low	Medium	High
Summary			
1. Do the program practices fit with my/our philosophy of early childhood education?	Low	Medium	High
2. Are the program practices and associated outcomes acceptable to us?	Low	Medium	High

Figure 2.2. Quality indicator questionnaire for defining the process of inclusion.

the quality of inclusion that can be used in more formal and summative program evaluations.

Evaluating the quality of inclusive programs is a difficult issue. We cannot advocate a cookie-cutter approach to inclusion. Children and families have different needs, and those needs must be met within the context of the community. Family needs such as the need for child care, the desire to have a child in a program in their neighborhood, or the desire to have a child in a program with staff that speak their native language, must all be considered when evaluating the quality of any early childhood program. Just as inclusion is not only about disability, quality cannot be only about inclusion. Inclusion is a necessary, but not a sufficient, component of a high-quality early childhood program. As we develop, implement, and evaluate inclusive programs, we need to consider the following issues:

- Inclusive programs belong to the community—that is, the families and staff who use and work in the program. The community must define inclusion in a manner that makes sense to its members.
- Programs need to be flexible enough to meet the needs of diverse children and families. Inclusion is not a one-size-fits-all endeavor.
- There are some common components that must be evaluated across programs. These include program philosophy, program organization, and curriculum.
- The bottom line of inclusive programs is how they meet the developmental and social needs of children with disabilities. Even if a program has an eloquent philosophy statement and elaborate organizational chart, if the needs of children are not met, it is not a high-quality inclusive program.

REFERENCES

Allen, K. E., & Schwartz, I. S. (2001). *The exceptional child: Inclusion in early childhood education.* Albany, NY: Delmar.

Division for Early Childhood. (2000). *Position statement on inclusion.* Available on website: http://www.dec-sped.org/positions/inclusio.html

Guralnick, M. J. (Ed.). (2000). *Early childhood inclusion: Focus on change.* Baltimore, MD: Brookes.

Stainback, W., & Stainback, S. (1990). *Support networks for inclusive schooling: Interdependent integrated education.* Baltimore, MD: Brookes.

Wolery, M. R., Pauca, T., Brashers, M., & Grant, S. (2000). *Quality of inclusive experiences measure.* Unpublished assessment manual, Frank Porter Graham Child Development Center, Chapel Hill, NC.

CHAPTER 3

Classroom Ecology and Child Participation

Samuel L. Odom,
William II. Brown, Ilene S. Schwartz,
Craig Zercher, & Susan R. Sandall

TIFFANY IS A 3½-YEAR-OLD, biracial child with bright brown eyes, straight brown hair usually swept up in a pony tail, and Down syndrome. She is attending the City Center Child Care program described in the previous chapter. Our field notes reported that Tiffany followed the classroom routines with little or no adult help. Although she was involved in activities with adults often and she spent much of her free-choice time in solitary play, she was an active participant in the class. As one example of this participation:

> Five children, ranging in age from six months to three years were in the room playing. Breakfast had just been delivered by John, an adult with disabilities that works at CCCC. Before anyone else went to the table, Tiffany went over and sat in the teacher's seat. It is a kidney-shaped table and the teacher spot was quite obvious. Using the spoons and bowls that arrived with breakfast Tiffany pretended to serve breakfast to people. As she served the food she was "talking" a mile a minute. (Schwartz, 1997, n.p.)

Jimmy was a 5-year-old boy with blond hair, blue eyes, and autism. He attended a class at the KidCorp Child Care Center, which was part of the network of community-based inclusive classes that made up the VIP program (see Appendix B for a description of this program). The teachers agreed that Jimmy had made great progress. When he began the year, he spent much of his time screaming and having tantrums. Several months later, a classroom assistant reported: "He could lie on his mat at naptime, line up and stand in line with other children, and allow the teacher to take him to the toilet" (Horn, Odom, Marquart, Pallas, & Kaiser, 1995, p. 37). However, an observer noted in her field notes:

> when he is in unstructured situations and when adults do not provide assistance in group activities, Jimmy often does not participate . . . Jimmy will often wander from one set of materials to another, sit on the floor alone, and stare into space. (Horn et al., 1995, p. 37)

For example, during a free-choice time:

> Valerie [the teacher] noticed that Jimmy was not doing anything, led him over to the blocks, and sat him down. Jimmy took two

blocks, pushed them on the floor a little, put them in his lap briefly, and then put them down, staring into space. He'd look up and then look down, touching the blocks. He clapped his hands and put his fingers in his ears. (field notes)

Our observations told us that Jimmy actively participated in classroom activities and routines only 26% of the time he was in class.

These two examples illustrate the range of children's participation in the inclusive preschool classrooms we observed. In early childhood education, child participation is an important concept (Bredekamp & Copple, 1997). We assume that children learn and develop by actively participating in developmentally appropriate settings. In our research, we were interested in describing both the amount of participation in inclusive programs for children with disabilities and typically developing children, as well as the early childhood environments, or ecologies, in which children participated. More specifically, we were interested in how certain features of the classroom ecology were associated with child participation and other, more specific types of child behaviors. The questions we addressed in this part of our research were:

- What do inclusive classrooms look like?
- What do children do in inclusive settings?
- Does it matter who initiates the activity?
- Do child characteristics, such as autism, affect children's engagement and other features of the classroom ecology?
- Is child participation different in programs with different organizational contexts and using different individualized service models?

Before describing what we found about these questions, it is important to briefly describe what we mean by some of the terms we use.

WHAT DO WE MEAN BY CLASS ECOLOGY AND CHILD PARTICIPATION?

When we talk about *classroom ecology*, we mean the physical and social characteristics of the classroom environment (Odom & Bailey, 2000). The physical characteristics could include the space in the classroom and how it is arranged, activities/routines/schedules, the initiator of activities (e.g., child, adult), the number of children in the class, and also the number of adults. Social characteristics are the interactions between teachers and children and the interactions among peers in the class.

When we refer to *child participation*, we mean the nature and degree to which children engage in social exchanges, activities, events, routines, and rituals in a variety of contexts (Schwartz, Sandall, Odom, Li, & Wolfberg, 1997). We will use the terms *participation* and *engagement* synonomously in this chapter. Note that our definition of engagement specifies *active* physical involvement in activities (e.g., building with blocks, pretend play) and class routines (e.g., walking in line to the gym; washing hands before snack) (Odom & Bailey, 2000). This definition is conservative in that it does not include children's attention to adults or other children as part of participation/engagement (e.g., watching a teacher talk during circle time, listening to a story, or watching a videotape). When other researchers talk about engagement, they sometimes include children looking at teachers and peers (McWilliam & Bailey, 1992).

WHAT DO INCLUSIVE PRESCHOOL CLASSROOMS LOOK LIKE?

As a first step in our research, it was important for us to describe the ecological features of the classrooms we studied, as well as the type of child participation occurring in those classrooms. As part of the ecological systems study, we observed 112 children for 30 minutes, on six different occasions. We used the CASPER, a quantitative observational assessment (see Appendix A), to record information about seven features of the classroom ecology (Brown, Odom, & Favazza, 1995).

1. Group arrangement—number of children and adults in a group
2. Group composition—proportion of children with and without disabilities in a group
3. Activity—the classroom area in which the child was located
4. Activity initiator—the individual who selected the activity in which the child was located (i.e., the teacher, the child, or a peer)
5. Adult behavior—support, approval, or comments to the child or group
6. Child behavior—physical participation in activities or routines
7. Child social behavior—social interaction with adults or peers

The research methods followed in this study and a more specific description of the findings appeared in Brown, Odom, Li, and Zercher (1999). The first five features are discussed in the next section, with the remaining two taken up in a subsequent section.

Group Arrangement and Composition

In inclusive classes, children with and without disabilities spent about the same amount of time in solitary or small-group activities with an adult, and in large-group activities. The children with disabilities spent more time in one-to-one activities with an adult (8% of their time vs. 2%), and the typically developing children spent more time in independent, small-group activities. When we looked at the group composition, we found that children with disabilities spent more time in "no group with peers" than did typically developing children (17% vs. 8%), due partly to the amount of time spent with an adult one-on-one. One way of telling that children with disabilities were becoming members of the class was to observe how often they were in integrated groups (i.e., groups that included children with and without disabilities) and segregated groups. We found that children both with and without disabilities were in integrated groups most of the time (73% and 61%, respectively), with typically developing children located in segregated groups more often because there were more of these children in the classrooms. The engagement of children in adult- and child-initiated activities is discussed later in this chapter.

Activities and Activity-Initiators

The activities in the class were remarkably similar for children with and without disabilities (see Figure 3.1). Children from both groups spent the majority of their time in circle time/group time, large motor, snack/food, transition, and manipulative (fine motor) activities.

In early childhood education, great value is placed on children's choice of activities in classes rather than on having adults constantly directing where children should go and what they should do (Bredekamp & Copple, 1997; Sandall, McLean, & Smith, 2000). For children with and without disabilities, activities were initiated more often by adults (57% and 54% of classroom time), but there were also substantial percentages of child-initiated activity (42% and 44%, respectively). Overall, this suggested a balance between the two types of activities, although it is important to note that there were variations across some classrooms. For example, at the Child Company Center in the VIP program

> Children appear to spend a inordinate amount of time sitting in assigned seats at tables. The teacher often reads a book while she sits in a chair opposite the tables . . . sitting for an hour without opportunity to wiggle was not uncommon (Horn et al., 1995, p. 30)

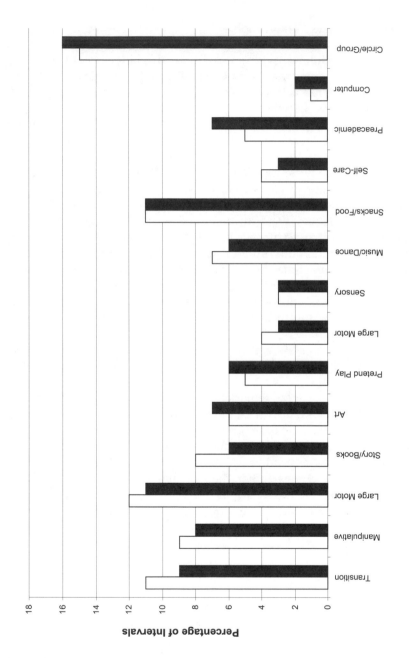

Figure 3.1. Percentage of intervals in which children with disabilities (white bars) and without disabilities (black bars) were located in different activity areas.

In this classroom, teacher-initiated activities occurred 97% of the time. In contrast, the classroom at the Wesley Center Child Care Center, also part of the VIP program, was very child-directed. The director said, "They [the children] learn by being provided lots of fresh materials in [a] child-directive format . . . so I really don't see much need at all to the teacher-directed . . . programming (Horn et al., 1995, p. 31). The teachers had several center times in which children chose from a number of activities. In this program, child-initiated activities occurred 67% of the time.

Adult Behavior

One part of the classroom ecology for young children is the social behavior that adults direct to children. Adults may provide support, approval, and/or comments directly to a child, or they may lead group activities in which their interactions are spread across several children in the classroom. In our observations, we found that teachers provided support to the children with disabilities nearly three times as much as they did to typically developing children (15% vs. 5% of their total time). For example, in Jimmy's classroom, the children are getting ready to go outside.

> Valerie [the teacher] tells Jimmy to go get his coat. She gestures to him also, but he gets up with Beth's [assistant teacher] assistance, and starts toward his cubbie. He gets halfway there. B. gives him another prompt and he goes to the cubbie. B. hands him his coat. She very patiently waits while he puts the coat on. Then she zips it up and gives him a hug. (field notes)

As can be seen in this example, teachers also provided approval and affection for children (i.e., B. giving Jimmy a hug), but from our CASPER observations, this was not substantially different for children with and without disabilities, and did not occur very often (2.2% and .62% of the time, respectively). The largest amount of adult behavior was group discussion/directions, which, again, was not different for the two groups (20.9% and 26.1%, respectively).

WHAT DID CHILDREN DO IN INCLUSIVE SETTINGS?

Children's participation was measured by their active engagement in specific behavior, which we also grouped into a summary measure of engagement. Also, we observed separately children's social engagement with peers and with adults.

Children's Participation in the Classroom

Children with and without disabilities engaged in very similar types of behavior in the inclusive settings. (Please note that we are reporting individual child behavior in the text rather than in a graph, for the sake of brevity. We do display child behavior occurring in teacher- and child-initiated activities in graphs in a later section.) Most often, children engaged in manipulating objects (19% and 15% of the time, respectively), self-care (10% for each group), and large motor behavior (8% and 7%). Reading or looking at books, singing/dancing, preacademic behavior, engaging in art, and pretend playing occurred a small but consistent amount of time (2–5%). In programs that provided children with choices of activities in which to participate, we would expect that children would spend their time in this range of activities. Games with rules, which are developmentally advanced behaviors (Smilansky, 1968), occurred infrequently, and clean-up, as we might expect, also occurred a small percentage of the time.

To gain a measure of children's overall participation, we grouped the individual child behaviors into a composite engagement score. Other researchers have proposed that children's amount of engagement in early childhood education settings is a measure of the quality of the setting (McWilliam, Trivette, & Dunst, 1985; Raspa, McWilliam, & Ridley, in press). On the CASPER, children with and without disabilities were engaged about the same amount of time (54% vs. 58%, respectively). Using peers' engagement as a comparison, this told us that children with disabilities were participating in classroom activities about as much as typically developing children. However, it is also important to remember that these global figures are only an average, and that individual children, like Tiffany and Jimmy, were engaged in very different levels of participation. We have begun to analyze how different types of child characteristics are related to engagement and also how the classroom ecology affects engagement. Several of these analyses are presented in subsequent sections of this chapter.

Children's Social Behavior

Because we discuss social behavior in more detail in Chapter 5, we will describe our findings briefly here. Children with disabilities directed social behavior to adults about twice as often as typically developing children (11.4% vs. 6.3%). This could have been because children with disabilities were in one-to-one groups with adults more often or because they were receiving more adult support. Also we found that typically developing children directed positive social behavior to peers (13.7% vs. 5.3% of the time) and received positive behavior from peers (4.4% vs. 2.5%) more often than children with disabilities. There were no differences in negative social behavior, which was very low for each group (i.e., less than 1% of the observations).

The difference in the amount of social interaction with peers by children with and without disabilities is similar to findings of other researchers (Guralnick, 1999) and could be because of several factors. First, children with disabilities may not be as competent in engaging their peers in social interaction (McConnell & Odom, 1999). Second, they may at times be socially rejected by peers (see Chapter 5 for a full discussion of this issue) and excluded from social interaction. Third, as noted above, children with disabilities, for whatever reason, are more often involved in interactions with adults. They were in one-to-one groups more often than typically developing children and received adult support more often. In our analyses of these data (Zercher, Odom, & Brown, in preparation), we found that when children interacted with adults, they were less likely to interact with peers. This does not mean that adults should avoid promoting social interaction among children with and without disabilities or should limit substantially their interactions with children. They just have to be aware of this correlation and be wise about what they do and say with children in the classroom, if a goal is to promote peer social interaction for certain children.

DOES IT MATTER WHO INITIATES THE ACTIVITY?

As noted previously, in early childhood education and now in special education, a great value is placed on allowing children to choose the activities in which they participate. We have described these in the CASPER as child-initiated activities. However, a concern may arise that adults may need to provide more support in order for children with disabilities to become engaged. This additional support may mean that adults more often select the activities in which children are placed. We have defined these as adult-initiated activities. In our research, we were interested in learning whether the initiator of the children's activities is related to engagement for children with and without disabilities.

To answer this question, we compared engagement for children with and without disabilities when adults selected the activity in which children were to be located (e.g., the teacher says, "Kevin, you need to go to circle time now") and when children choose the activity in which they would be located (e.g., without teacher directions, Kevin sits down in the block area). This information appears in Figure 3.2. As shown there, the findings were similar for both groups of children. When children with and without disabilities selected the activities, they were engaged nearly 70% of the time, and when adults chose activities for children, children were engaged between 45% and 49% of the time. In other research outside the ECRII project, we found this same relationship (i.e., children are more engaged in child-initiated than in adult-initiated activities) (Odom et al., 2001; Odom, Favazza, Brown, & Horn, 2000).

The greater engagement in child-initiated activities is presumed to be a good thing. It is possible, however, that in adult-initiated activities, children may be engaging in different types of behavior than occur in child-initiated activities. The graphs in Figures 3.3a and 3.3b show the different child behaviors occurring in child-initiated and adult-initiated activities for children with and without disabilities. For both groups of children, books, music, self-help, and, to a small extent, preacademic behaviors occurred more often in adult-initiated activities. In child-initiated activities, pretend play, manipulative, and large motor behaviors

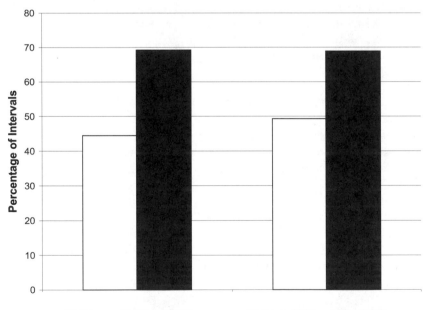

Figure 3.2. Engagement in adult-initiated activities (white bars) and child-initiated activities (black bars) for children with and without disabilities.

appeared more often. This information suggests that both child- and adult-initiated activities support or provide the opportunity for different types of behaviors, so a balance between the two types of activities makes sense.

In summary, these findings tell us that children with disabilities participate as much in inclusive preschool classes as do typically developing children, and both groups of children will be more engaged in child-initiated than in adult-initiated activities. In child-initiated activities, children engage in behaviors that may lead to learning and development—that is, pretend play, fine motor behaviors, large motor activity, and to some extent art. However, there are other behaviors that may lead to other forms of learning and development and that occur more often in adult-initiated activities—books and stories, preacademic behavior, music, and to some extent self-care. Although children's overall engagement may occur less often in these activities, they still are important learning experiences and qualitatively different from the experiences occurring in child-initiated activities. Recommended practices in early childhood education specify that there should be a balance between child- and adult-directed activity, but until now this recommendation has been based on theory rather than empirical findings. We feel that our research provides an empirical basis for this recommendation.

DO CHILD CHARACTERISTICS AFFECT CHILDREN'S EXPERIENCES OF THE CLASSROOM ECOLOGY?

From our field notes, it was apparent that features of the classroom ecology and children's engagement were different for children having different characteristics. Other authors have written about how individual children in the same classroom can have very different experiences and behave very differently (Carta, Sainato, & Greenwood, 1988). We have begun looking at how children with different characteristics may experience and participate in inclusive preschool settings differently. Because today there is a great deal of discussion about appropriate programming for children with autism (Rogers, 1999), and because children with autism often have very severe impairments in a range of skills, we began our research with this group.

Of the 80 children with disabilities in our ecological systems study, 10 children were identified as having autism or pervasive developmental disorder (PDD). For each of the 10 children with autism/PDD, we selected another child with disabilities with similar characteristics, except for disability category, and a typically developing child from the same class (Odom, Brown, Zercher, & Tsao, 2001). This gave us a group of 30 children.

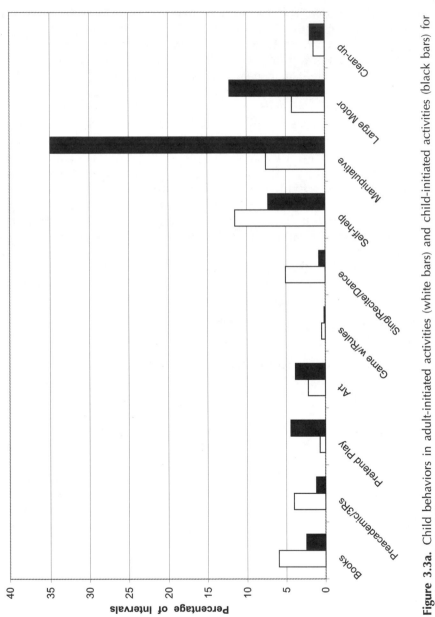

Figure 3.3a. Child behaviors in adult-initiated activities (white bars) and child-initiated activities (black bars) for children with disabilities.

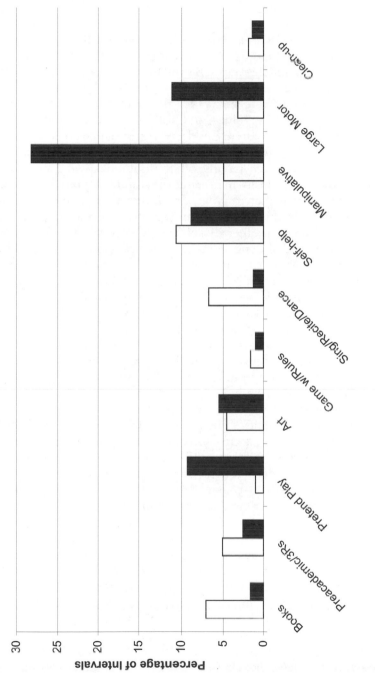

Figure 3.3b. Child behaviors in adult-initiated activities (white bars) and child-initiated activities (black bars) for children without disabilities.

We found that children with autism tended to be in solitary and one-to-one activities with adults more often than the other two groups of children, and were less often in small-group activities only with peers (this information is reported in the text rather than graphically). Adult support and interactions with adults were similar for the children with autism/PDD and children with other disabilities, and both were greater than occurred for typically developing children. Children with autism were in transition and manipulative activities more often than the other two groups of children, while the children having other disabilities were more often (than the children with autism) in pretend play, and the typically developing children were more often in preacademic activities (than either of the other two groups). In this substudy, engagement for the children with autism and children with other disabilities was very similar (51% and 52%, respectively), with the engagement for typically developing children quite a bit higher (59%). Not surprisingly, for the children with autism in contrast to the children with other disabilities and typically developing children, social behavior to peers (3% vs. 9% vs. 14%) and social behavior from peers (2% vs. 4% vs. 6%) were much lower. Again, negative behavior to peers or adults did not occur very often.

In summary, we have learned from this beginning analysis that children with different characteristics, in this case autism, experience the ecology of the same program differently. They may engage in different specific behaviors, but in the inclusive preschool programs in which we observed, overall engagement did not appear to be different from that of other children with disabilities, although it was lower than that of typically developing children. As reflective of one of the primary impairments related to the disability, children with autism were much less socially engaged than other children in their classrooms.

To look more closely at characteristics of children with disabilities and child participation, investigators at each of our sites selected children with disabilities who had high and low levels of engagement (as measured by the CASPER), regardless of the disability classification (Schwartz et al., 1997). We then developed short case studies for each student and examined the differences between these two types of children. Across the sites, children with high and low levels of engagement had different disabilities. Children with higher participation tended to be involved more often in child-initiated activities, which is similar to the findings reported in the previous section. Children with low levels of participation spent more time alone, although not generally more time in one-to-one activities with the teacher. For children with low and high levels of participation, there was no difference in adult support. Children with high participation tended to be more outgoing, especially in interactions with the teacher, and some tended to participate in a limited number of activities in which they were very engaged. For children with low levels of participation, disruptive behaviors (which were at a very low percentage for all children) tended to interfere with engagement. One conclusion from this study was that teacher support, which occurred a similar amount of time for both groups of children, may not have been effective for the children with low participation. For these children, more individualized forms of teacher support may be needed. Last, the highest rates of engagement appeared to occur in familiar classroom routines and rituals. Incorporating familiar activities, routines, and schedules in classrooms where they do not exist may well support the engagement of children.

HOW DO ORGANIZATIONAL CONTEXTS AND INDIVIDUALIZED SERVICE MODELS AFFECT CHILD PARTICIPATION?

In our study, we grouped the inclusive programs we observed according to organizational contexts (the agencies or organizations within which the inclusive classes were located) and individualized-service models (how educational services were provided to children with disabilities) (see Figure A.1 in Appendix A). Given these differences, it would be important to see if child participation was dramatically different in the different contexts. Our ability to answer these questions was limited by the small number of programs with which we worked, so our findings cannot be viewed as being applicable to all other settings. However, they do provide some insights into the programs with which we worked.

In Figure 3.4, we grouped the programs into three of the organizational contexts mentioned before, Head Start (5 programs), community-based (2 programs), and public school (9 programs). In general, children with disabilities appeared to be most engaged in Head Start inclusive programs, with engagement occurring a little less in the community-based programs, and quite a bit less in the public school programs. For typically developing children, engagement was nearly equal in the Head Start and community-based programs, but quite a bit less in the public school programs.

In Figure 3.5, we present child engagement in the different individualized-service models. Children with disabilities appeared to be most engaged in the itinerant-collaborative, itinerant-direct service, early childhood, and early childhood special education (ECSE) models. Engagement occurred less often in the team teaching model and least in the integrative-activities model. In comparison with typically developing children, the children with disabilities appeared to be substantially less engaged in the

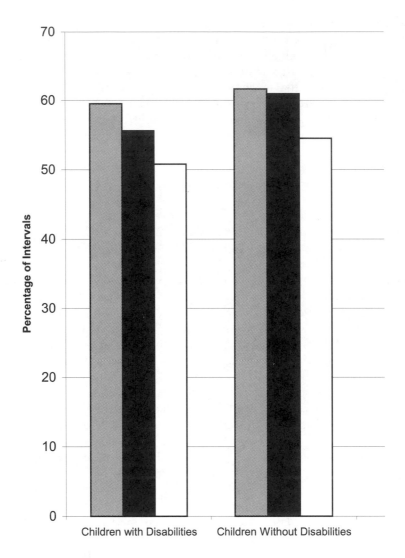

Figure 3.4. Engagement in different organizational contexts for children with and without disabilities. Gray bars indicate Head Start programs; black bars indicate community-based programs; white bars indicate public school programs.

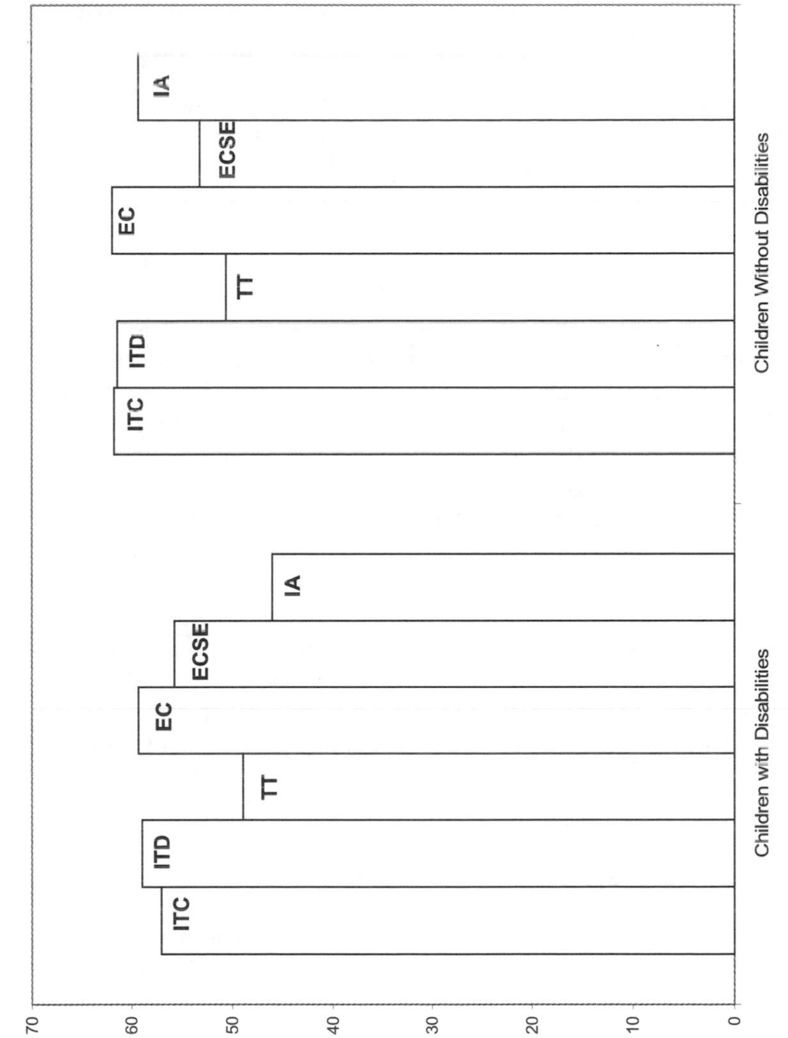

Figure 3.5. Engagement in different individualized service models for children with and without disabilities. Models were classified as itinerant-collaborative (ITC), itinerant direct service (ITD), team teaching (TT), early childhood (EC), reverse mainstreaming (ECSE), and integrative activities (IA).

integrative-activities model, and somewhat more engaged in the early childhood special education model.

In summary, both Head Start and community-based models did appear to be more supportive of child participation for children with and without disabilities. Child participation appeared to occur less in public school contexts, but this may well be because of the individualized-service models that appeared only in public school contexts (integrative activities, ECSE, and team teaching). The quality of the early childhood environment (at least as suggested by child participation) in these organizational contexts certainly needs further study.

Also, these findings suggest that for children with disabilities, engagement in settings in which they are receiving itinerant services, and in early childhood settings in which few special education services were provided, was at least equivalent to that in settings having a greater special education orientation (e.g., ECSE and integrative activities). We were surprised that engagement was somewhat lower in the team teaching classes. This individualized-service model has great potential for supporting children with disabilities because a special education teacher would be in the classroom all the time. Other researchers have found team teaching to be a very effective model (McCormick, Noonan, & Heck, 1998) for supporting children's engagement. The degree to which this model works well for children and adults depends in part on the collaborative relationship established between teachers (see Chapter 6) and the teachers' beliefs about individualizing learning opportunities for young children with disabilities (Lieber et al., 1998).

IMPLICATIONS FOR PRACTICE

Our research on classroom ecology and child participation was descriptive (rather than experimental), so the implications of this research for practice should be viewed as suggestive rather than conclusive. Given that caution, these findings tell us several things.

- Overall, the inclusive settings appear to support the engagement of children with disabilities at least as well as they support the engagement of typically developing children. The features of the classroom ecology (e.g., activities, group arrangements) appear to be similar for the two groups of children. However, children with disabilities did receive three times the amount of adult support as typically developing children. Teachers in inclusive preschool classes should be aware that additional support may be necessary for fostering child engagement of some children with disabilities.

- Although children in general were more engaged in child-initiated than in adult-initiated activities, the child behaviors occurring in the two types of activities were different. These findings support the general practice in regular early childhood education and special education of balancing child- and adult-directed activities in inclusive preschool classrooms.

- Children in our study (both with and without disabilities) were somewhat more engaged in regular early childhood programs (community preschool, Head Start) than in public school programs. We expect with the right personnel and circumstances, public school programs are as effective in supporting child engagement as the other two contexts (for example, average engagement in a Lincoln County program—a public school program—was a respectable 56%). However, the hesitance of administrators to place children with disabilities in regular early childhood settings because of concern about their participation in the program did not appear to be supported by our findings.

- Children with different characteristics engaged in the early childhood setting differently. As expected, children with autism/PDD were less socially engaged in the settings, but their overall activity engagement did not differ from that of other children with disabilities (and was below that of typically developing children). In addition, at each of our research sites, we could identify children who were "low engagers." We noted the importance of having familiar classroom activities, routines, and rituals for supporting the engagement of these children with disabilities. More specialized interventions and supports also may be needed. We describe such accommodations and intervention approaches in Chapter 4. However, an implication for teachers is that they should directly monitor the engagement of children with disabilities (and perhaps some of the children without disabilities) in their classrooms. When child engagement occurs infrequently (children move between activities often and do not become involved when they are in an activity), teachers should plan ways of supporting the participation of children.

In conclusion, the features of a classroom's ecology and their effect on child behavior are complex, but important to understand. Our research very much reflects the reciprocal influences suggested in Bronfenbrenner's ecological systems approach described in Chapter 1. That is, there are features of the classroom ecology that appear to affect child behaviors (e.g., the extent to which classrooms are adult-directed), but there are also characteristics of the child and his/her behavior that may affect the classroom ecology (e.g., the amount of adult support provided to children with disabilities compared with typically developing children). It is important for teachers to be aware of these reciprocal influences when planning their classroom activities and teaching.

REFERENCES

Bredekamp, S., & Copple, C. (Eds.). (1997). *Developmentally appropriate practice in early childhood programs* (rev. ed.). Washington, DC: National Association for the Education of Young Children.

Brown, W. H., Odom, S. L., & Favazza, P. C. (1995). *Code for Active Student Participation and Engagement Revised (CASPER II)*. Observer training manual, Vanderbilt University, Early Childhood Research Institute on Inclusion, Nashville, TN.

Brown, W. H., Odom, S. L., Li, S., & Zercher, C. (1999). Ecobehavioral assessment in early childhood programs: A portrait of preschool inclusion. *Journal of Special Education, 33*, 138–153.

Carta, J. J., Sainato, D. M., & Greenwood, C. R. (1988). Advances in ecological assessment of classroom instruction for young children with handicaps. In S. Odom & M. Karnes (Eds.), *Early intervention for infants and children with handicaps* (pp. 317–340). Baltimore, MD: Brookes.

Guralnick, M. J. (1999). The nature and meaning of social integration for young children with mild developmental delays in inclusive settings. *Journal of Early Intervention, 22*, 70–86.

Horn, E., Odom, S. L., Marquart, J., Pallas, P., & Kaiser, A. (1995). *Stepping out into the community: VIP case study*. Unpublished case study, Vanderbilt University, Early Childhood Research Institute on Inclusion, Nashville, TN.

Lieber, J., Capell, K., Sandall, S. R., Wolfberg, P., Horn, E., & Beckman, P. J. (1998). Inclusive preschool programs: Teachers' beliefs and practices. *Early Childhood Research Quarterly, 13*, 87–105.

McConnell, S. R., & Odom, S. L. (1999). Performance-based assessment of social competence for young children with disabilities. Development and initial evaluation of a multi-measure model. *Topics in Early Childhood Special Education, 19*, 67–74.

McCormick, L., Noonan, M. J., & Heck, R. (1998). Variables affecting engagement in inclusive preschool classrooms. *Journal of Early Intervention, 21*, 160–176.

McWilliam, R. A., & Bailey, D. B. (1992). Promoting engagement and mastery. In D. B. Bailey & M. Wolery (Eds.), *Teaching infants and preschoolers with disabilities* (pp. 229–255). Columbus, OH: Merrill.

McWilliam, R. A., Trivette, C. M., & Dunst, C. J. (1985). Behavior engagement as a measure of efficacy of early intervention. *Analysis and Intervention in Developmental Disabilities, 5*, 59–71.

Odom, S. L., & Bailey, D. B. (2000). Inclusive preschool programs: Ecology and child outcomes. In M. Guralnick (Ed.), *Early childhood inclusion: Focus on change* (pp. 253–276). Baltimore, MD: Brookes.

Odom, S. L., Brown, W. H., Skellenger, A., Ostrosky, M., Tsao, L., & Haynes, D. (2001). *The relationship of activity-initiator and child engagement in preschool classrooms for children with and without disabilities.* Unpublished manuscript.

Odom, S. L., Brown, W. H., Zercher, C., & Tsao, L. (2001). *Child with autism/ PDD in inclusive preschool settings: Classroom ecology and child participation.* Unpublished manuscript.

Odom, S. L., Favazza, P. C., Brown, W. H., & Horn, E. M. (2000). Approaches to understanding the ecology of inclusive early childhood settings for children with disabilities. In T. Thompson, D. Felce, & F. Symons (Eds.), *Behavioral observation: Innovations in technology and application in developmental disabilities* (pp. 193–214). Baltimore, MD: Brookes.

Raspa, S. M., McWilliam, R. A., & Ridley, S. M. (in press). Child care quality and children's engagement. *Early Education and Development.*

Rogers, S. (1999). Intervention for young children with autism: From research to practice. *Infants and Young Children, 12*(2), 1–16.

Sandall, S., McLean, M. E., & Smith, B. J. (2000). *DEC recommended practices in early intervention/early childhood special education.* Longmont, CO: Sopris West.

Schwartz, I. S. (1997). *Child participation case study—Field notes.* Unpublished case study, University of Washington, Early Childhood Research Institute on Inclusion, Seattle.

Schwartz, I., Sandall, S., Odom, S. L., Li, S., & Wolfberg, P. (1997, April). *Child participation in inclusive preschool classrooms.* Paper presented at the Biennial Conference of the Society for Research in Child Development, Washington, DC.

Smilansky, S. (1968). *The effects of sociodramatic play on disadvantaged preschool children.* New York: Wiley.

Zercher, C., Odom, S. L., & Brown, W. H. (in preparation). *Social ecology of inclusive preschool settings.*

CHAPTER 4

Classroom Models of
Individualized Instruction

*Eva Horn, Joan Lieber, Susan R. Sandall,
Ilene S. Schwartz, & Ruth A. Wolery*

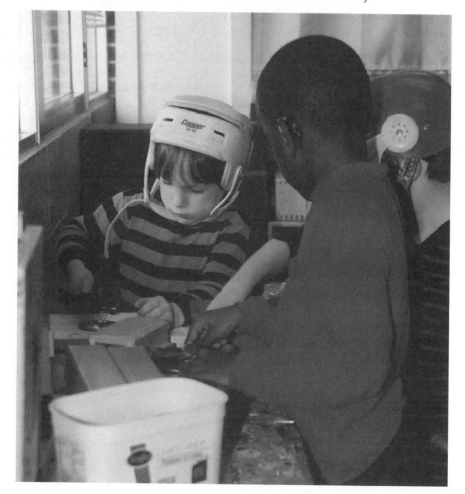

IT'S 8:00 A.M. AT THE BUTTERMILK STATION class in the Rolling Hills Head Start program. Ms. Catherine pins the children's names on the construction paper "helping hands" located on the bulletin board as the children eagerly volunteer for daily jobs. She puts Benny's name on the finger for being the "flag holder." Jessica will pass out the napkins. Sarah will be the "Benny helper." Now it's time to pledge allegiance to the flag. Sarah jumps up quickly to go to Benny. She rolls Benny, who is sitting in a chair secured to a platform on wheels, to the front of the room and turns him to face his peers. The teacher hands Benny the flag, which he proudly waves as he and his classmates recite the pledge of allegiance. (classroom observation)

Adaptations and supports like those provided to Benny were just a natural part of the everyday flow of activities in the Buttermilk Station Head Start class. All class members participated in the full range of activities offered and used essentially the same materials. Accommodations were readily made as needed for children with an identified disability.

For children with disabilities in inclusive settings, professionals agree that a high-quality early childhood classroom environment is the necessary foundation (Bailey, McWilliam, Buysse, & Wesley, 1998; Wolery & Bredekamp, 1994). However, placement and participation in a high-quality early childhood classroom alone might not provide a sufficient level of instruction for addressing the individual learning needs of children with disabilities (Carta, Schwartz, Atwater, & McConnell, 1991). An important function of an educational team for children with disabilities should be to develop goals and objectives that (1) meet the unique needs of the child, (2) are meaningful for the child, and (3) are functional in a variety of contexts (Notari-Syverson & Schuster, 1995). Supports to assist the child in reaching these goals should not take the place of the classroom curriculum or restrict the child's participation in classroom activities. Learning opportunities should take place within the context of the existing classroom routine.

Based on previous research, we know that early childhood teachers do not usually make major changes in the amount or type of activities in their classrooms based on the presence of children with disabilities (Wolery et al., 1994). Teachers do report that they modify and adapt classroom activities to meet the needs of individual children, but there is very little information about what these modifications and adaptations look like in inclusive early childhood programs. Goodman and Bond (1993) suggested that a child's IEP is viewed by some general educators as a separate and unrelated curriculum. Our participant observations and interviews with teachers confirmed this notion. The early childhood teacher frequently viewed the time the child spent with the itinerant teacher or specialist as the child's special education (Janko, Schwartz, Sandall, Anderson, & Cottam, 1997; Lieber et al., 1997). Further, early childhood teachers reported that they had limited access to the IEP process and/or the document. Even if the teachers made modifications to the curriculum to assist the child, they may or may not have been providing the instruction needed to address the child's individualized goals and objectives.

Investigators participating in the Early Childhood Research Institute on Inclusion were interested in learning how individualized instruction could be provided to young children with disabilities to ensure that they were making progress. The ecological systems study described in Chapter 1 allowed us to identify some of the adaptations and accommodations that teachers were making to support children's participation. Through a series of focus groups, we were able to take a closer look at the range and specific nature of these accommodations. Also, in another set of studies, we learned how to implement and support others in implementing a strategy called embedded learning opportunities (ELO), which provides more direct support than a modification or adaptation.

Before discussing these individualized instruction strategies, we need to clarify a frequently misunderstood term. *Individualized* does not necessarily mean providing a dedicated block of time for one-on-one repeated trial instruction. It does mean that adults, by creating regular and frequent teaching and learning episodes as a part of the ongoing routines and activities of the classroom curriculum, ensure that young children are making progress on their goals (Lieber, Schwartz, Sandall, Horn, & Wolery, 1999).

CURRICULUM MODIFICATIONS AND ADAPTATIONS

A series of focus groups allowed us to identify the range and types of curriculum modifications and adaptations that teachers make to support the active participation of young children with disabilities and typically developing children in the same classroom. Thirteen focus groups were conducted in each of the ECRII sites (located in California, Maryland, North Carolina, Tennessee, and Washington) with teachers and therapists who had experience in inclusive preschool classrooms. Participants generated 529 curriculum modifications and adaptations, which through content analysis procedures were grouped into eight categories. Results were then shared with expert groups for feedback, reduction, and validation. The methodology and specific findings of this study are reported in Sandall, Joseph, and colleagues (in press).

A curriculum modification or adaptation is a change in a classroom activity or material that allows a child to participate. Increased participation creates more opportunities for children to develop and learn. Teachers should use a curriculum modification strategy when the child is interested in the ongoing activities but is not able to fully participate. The child may watch the other children and may try to participate, but not succeed, or may not stay with the activity long enough. The key is to help the child participate. Members of our focus groups not only described the types of modifications they made but gave actual examples of the modifications. The eight types of curriculum modifications and adaptations were: environmental support, material adaptations, special equipment, use of children's preferences, simplification of the activity, adult support, peer support, and invisible support.

Three of the modification strategies address changing or adding materials or events within the classroom; that is, those things that are external to the child. By *environmental support*, we mean altering the physical, social, and temporal environment to promote participation, engagement, and learning. For example, if a child had a problem making transitions from one activity to the next, just before the transition the teacher could provide the child with a picture or symbol representing the area or activity that the child should go to next. The child could even take the picture card to the next area. *Material adaptations* occur when teachers modify materials so that the child can participate as independently as possible. Examples of material adaptations include stabilizing materials using tape, Velcro, or nonskid backing or using contact paper or other sticky paper as the backing for collages if gluing and pasting are too difficult. *Special equipment* is another modification. Special or adaptive equipment devices may be used that allow a child to participate or to increase a child's level of participation. These include homemade equipment or devices as well as commercially available therapeutic equipment. Using a beanbag chair on the floor to position a child who typically sits in an adaptive wheelchair so that the child sits with the other children is an example of using special equipment.

Two of the modification strategies focus on matching activities with the child's abilities and preferences: *use of children's preferences* and *simplification of the activity*. If the child is not taking advantage of the available opportunities, the adults identify child preferences and integrate them into the activity to make it more motivating. For example, a highly preferred toy could be placed in a center to which the child rarely goes. Simplifying a complicated activity by breaking it into smaller parts, or changing or reducing the steps involved, is the second strategy in this group. Here one might simply give the child materials for an activity, such as a puzzle, one piece at a time. The teacher also might use a version of this strategy with a child who plays repetitively, and rarely in multiple-step scenarios, within the house corner or dramatic play area. The teacher could make photographs of three or four step play scenes, arrange them in a sequence, show and explain them to the child, and guide the child through the sequence as a way of lengthening the child's play.

The final set of three modification strategies focuses on providing either *adult*, *peer*, or *invisible support* to the child. In adult support, a teacher may model an appropriate behavior, join the child in play, praise the child, and/or provide encouragement. A child, for example, may be dumping and filling a cup at the sand table over and over and over. The teacher could make a positive comment about the child's play (praising and providing encouragement) and then show the child how to turn the cup over slowly to create a "mound" (modeling). Together they could then create "a landscape of mounds." Peers also can help children with disabilities reach learning objectives. For example, teachers might use a buddy system for some activities and transitions, in which a peer could show a child how to make a birthday cake with Play-Doh or line up to go outside. Finally, invisible supports occur when teachers rearrange aspects of naturally occurring activities (e.g., child's turn, opportunity to use materials) to support the child's success in participating. A favorite example of ours provided by one of the focus-group participants was for a child with limitations in hand strength to be nearer the end of the line in scooping ice cream for making a sundae so that the ice cream has melted a bit and "scoops" with less effort.

These eight types of curriculum modifications generated through the focus-group study, together with the participants' specific examples, form the core of the curriculum modifications section of our teacher resource guide, *Building Blocks for Successful Early Childhood Programs: Strategies for Including All Children* (Sandall, Schwartz, et al., in press).

EMBEDDED LEARNING OPPORTUNITIES

Curriculum modifications, used well, can help achieve one goal of inclusion, that is, active participation of young children with disabilities and typically developing children in the same classroom. However, curriculum modifications may not be sufficient to ensure that the child has learning opportunities to meet the goals and objectives stated on the IEP. To address this problem, early childhood special education professionals have recommended embedding instruction into existing classroom activities and routines (Bricker & Cripe, 1992; Davis, Kilgo, & Gamel-McCormick, 1998; Noonan & McCormick, 1995; Wolery & Wilbers, 1994). Embedding is "a procedure in which children are given opportunities to practice individual goals and objectives that are included within an activity or event in a manner that expands, modifies or adapts the activity/event while remaining meaningful, and interesting to children" (Bricker, Pretti-Fronczak, & McComas, 1998, p. 13).

Drawing on our observations and interviews in the ecological systems study, previous research about instructional use of embedding (e.g., Fox & Hanline, 1993; Mudd & Wolery, 1987; Peck, Killen, & Baumgart, 1989; Venn & Wolery, 1992; Venn et al., 1993), and the developmental work by Bricker and colleagues related to activity-based interventions (Bricker et al., 1998), we designed a teaching strategy called embedded learning opportunities (ELO). ELO is based on the premise that although many early childhood education programs offer learning opportunities across the day, children with disabilities may need guidance and support in order to recognize and learn from those opportunities. Thus teachers should pick out times during the day when children can practice the skills stated in the IEP objectives in natural activities and routines occurring in the class. During those times, teachers should embed short but systematic teaching interactions that help the child successfully use the skill.

For example, rather than setting up special sessions for teaching "object labels," labeling objects can be taught in regular activities in the class, such as naming body parts during doll play, naming items of clothing during dress-up/dramatic play, or labeling foods and eating utensils during snack or snack preparation. If a refined grasp is a child's learning goal, teachers could provide practice opportunities by having the child grasp a raisin, apple slice, or cheese wedge during snack or pick up pieces of tape during art.

We focused on developing "user friendly" materials to help teachers systematically provide learning opportunities during natural routines and activities in the class. Adapting a nondirective consultation strategy (Peck, Killen, & Baumgart, 1989), we worked with teachers in three inclusive preschool programs to identify opportunities for embedded teaching. Specifically, we wanted to develop procedures for supporting early childhood teachers' use of ELO, to assess the teachers' use, and to describe their perceptions of ELO. Importantly, we collected information on the impact of ELO on children's behaviors.

After making the decision to use ELO, the various members of the child's support team (including the early childhood special education teacher and related service professionals) had to complete several steps. They were (1) modifying the learning objectives, if necessary, so that they could be implemented as a part of the preschool curriculum; (2) organizing the objectives into learning opportunities; and (3) designing, implementing, and evaluating the embedded instruction.

Step 1: Modifying the Learning Objectives for the Preschool Curriculum

The purpose of this step is to translate an objective from a child's IEP to a learning objective that can be taught effectively in the classroom. Here we focused on the importance of remembering that learning objectives are not the same thing as activities, and that planning an activity is not the same thing as providing instruction. For example, a child's learning objective might include such skills as reaching, grasping, nodding "yes," or responding to simple commands. These objectives are not themselves activities, but are skills that children are expected to use during real activities in order to be more successful. Thus the teacher and other members of the support team begin by focusing on an activity in which the child can use or practice the needed skill. This approach supports the child's understanding of how a skill would be used in different settings and with different materials and people.

In addition, the support team needs to realize that the way in which an objective is written actually may limit the potential for ELO. For example, an IEP objective of "object labeling" might be written as follows: "Child will correctly label 4 out of 5 pictures when asked, What is this?" When the objective is stated in this way, the skill is likely to be taught by the teacher sitting at a table with the child looking at pictures. If the objective is restated as: "Child will correctly label objects when asked, What is this? within ongoing activities," it is more likely to be taught by (1) hiding objects in various places (e.g., in drawers, boxes) and encouraging labeling as each is "discovered"; (2) labeling materials used in the "washing the baby" activity; and (3) naming utensils and objects needed to set up the table for snack time.

So, the three primary purposes of Step 1 are to ensure that objectives are conceptualized so that they still (1) can be embedded within the routines (e.g., arrival, snack, clean-up) and planned activities (e.g., water play, cooking, group games) of the preschool classroom; (2) can be embedded across multiple daily activities so that the child receives sufficient opportunities to practice the skill; and, finally and most important, (3) reflect the acquisition of new behaviors for the child, not just practice of already acquired behaviors. Sometimes that may require the support team to work on one part of an objective at a time.

Step 2: Organizing the Objectives into Learning Opportunities

To ensure that a child progresses in his or her learning objectives, teaching plans must create opportunities for the child to perform the behavior. For example:

> One of Alex's objectives is to increase the use of his walker and to increase the speed with which he moves from place to place. Alex, however, prefers to play tabletop games with his classmates during center time rather than practicing his walking. Taking both of these pieces of information into account, the teacher sets up the materials so that Alex must use his walker to go to the center shelves to get the table games, place them in a basket attached to his walker, and walker to the table where his friends are seated.

In addition to setting up opportunities, plans also must ensure that the child has multiple opportunities to practice objectives within and across daily activities. For example:

> Because increasing Alex's "speed" of travel with his walker is an important aspect of his learning objective, the teacher initially makes careful notes about the various transition opportunities occurring throughout the day (arrival and putting away belongings; toileting and self-care; movement between centers, snack time, etc.). She also notes how long it currently takes Alex to complete these transitions. She then establishes transition "start times" for Alex that require him to move slightly faster than he currently does in order to arrive at the next activity concurrently with his peers. Alex now has multiple opportunities to practice the objective that "pushes" his proficient use of the walker.

To support the teacher in accomplishing these two important components (setting up learning opportunities and creating multiple learning opportunities) of organizing the learning objectives for each child, we designed the two forms shown in Figure 4.1. The first, "IEP-at-a-Glance," is a shorthand reference for each child's IEP objectives. This reference provides on one page a one- to three-word description of the objectives, a brief description of the child's current abilities, and any specific information on special management needs the child might require. The second form

IEP-at-a-Glance

Child's Name: *Alex*	**Age:** *48 mos.* **Date:** *9/02*

Objectives in a Word: *Two signs together* *Matching/sorting* *Follow 2-step directions* *Pincer grasp* *Walks across elevation changes* *Toileting on schedule* **Management Needs:** *Uses grunts and pointing to* *communicate, can easily get* *frustrated, and yells and stomps feet*	**Child Profile:** *Beginning to communicate verbally* *but continues to use sign language* *and verbal approximations (wa for* *water). Uses 25 single signs* *consistently (e.g., eat, drink, Mom,* *book, toy, want, stop, more, play,* *finish, sleep, cookie, water, out,* *music, computer). Can walk well* *but has problems transitioning* *across changes in elevation. Tends* *to play side-by-side with peers* *rather than initiating play.*

Activity Matrix for Alex

	Skills to be Taught					
Activity	**Signs**	**Matching**	**Directions**	**Grasp**	**Elevations**	**Toileting**
Arrival	Greeting teacher and peers; saying goodbye to Mom		As direction needed, provide in 2 steps	Hang coat on hook, unzip backpack	Step up to cubby	Provide opportunity —stay dry through next activity
Circle	Response to questions	Matching colors, shapes, pictures	With pictures/ books/action songs	Picking up items for finger play, musical instruments	Stepping over small obstacle on path to group circle	Staying dry through activity
Clean-up	What to clean and where	Matching objects to photo		Grasping small items to put away	Step up to shelves	Provide opportunity

Figure 4.1. IEP-at-a-Glance and activity matrix for Alex. *Note.* Reprinted with permission from *Building Blocks for Successful Early Childhood Programs,* by S. Sandall et al., in press, Baltimore, MD: Brookes.

is an individual child activity matrix. The activity matrix is designed to describe and reflect the many opportunities to embed objectives through-out the daily program schedule.

Step 3: Designing, Implementing, and Evaluating Embedded Instruction

Activities alone, even when they are fun and engaging, do not guarantee that children will learn and use the skills described in their IEP objectives. Nor does simply creating an opportunity ensure that the child will achieve the learning objectives. The opportunity must be paired with instruction. Good embedded instructions must let the children know (1) what they need to do, (2) how a "correct" response looks and feels, (3) the "correct-ness" of their response, and (4) that a response will result in a positive outcome. The teacher must plan carefully for each learning objective how these four parts of the learning equation will occur to support the child's learning of the "new" skill. It is also crucial that the teacher systematically monitor the child's progress. It is from this monitoring that the teacher can determine when the child no longer needs instructional support or whether the plan needs to be modified because it is not resulting in the child's learning the needed skill. The "Program-at-a Glance" (modification from McCormick & Feeney, 1995) form is a useful organizing tool to accomplish these instructional planning components (see Figure 4.2).

EVALUATING THE ELO PROCEDURE

To determine whether the procedures we had developed were in fact useful for teachers, we observed and interviewed teachers in inclusive preschool classrooms (Horn, Lieber, Li, Sandall, & Schwartz, 2000). We monitored the teachers' use of ELO and the subsequent effect on the child's learning objectives. Also, we asked teachers to describe their perception of the ELO teaching approach and effects on children. The information helped us modify and revise the procedures.

All teachers with whom we worked increased their use of the embed-ded teaching approach. Children also increased their use of the skills in the learning objectives. In follow-up interviews, teachers reported generally favorable perceptions of the ELO procedures. We found, however, that the teachers' ongoing use of the ELO strategy depended on the nature of the target objective and on how instruction was delivered in the classroom. For example, an IEP objective such as "pouring with minimal spillage" was easier to embed and support in a natural activity flow than was "increasing verbal responsiveness" in a large-group choral responding

Program-at-a-Glance for: _Alex_

Objective: _Pour liquid or other fluid material (e.g., sand, beans) from one container into another without spillage._

Date: _8/14_   **Activity:** _Centers_   **Material:** _All centers available_

Modifications Needed:

*__*Water table__: Add a variety of containers with spouts (plastic measuring cups, teapot, play pitcher)*

*__*Snack Center__: Add pouring juice for other children to workjobs*

*__*Housekeeping:__ Add beans to kitchen cabinet in a small pitcher for pouring into pots, cups, or plates*

*__*Art Center:__ Place tempera paint in small pitcher, have children pour into individual bowls*

What are you going to do?

Move through center modeling use of these new activities/materials
Provide physical guidance for Alex

What are you going to say?

Use natural cues—Let's see you do it. Can you do it and get all the beans into the pot?

How will you respond?

Praise, acknowledgment, feedback on accuracy, engagement in activity created

Evaluation Procedures:

Who? _Jane and Sue_   **Where?** _Snack & art_   **When?** _Weekly_
How? ___Narrative Summary   ___Portfolio   _✓_Observation

Keep tally using following coding schemes—I (independent and correct), P (independent but only partially correct), H (needed assistance), W (incorrect)

Figure 4.2. Program-at-a-Glance for Alex. *Note.* Reprinted with permission from *Building Blocks for Successful Early Childhood Programs,* by S. Sandall et al., in press, Baltimore, MD: Brookes.

activity. We also found that teachers' beliefs about their role in supporting children's learning determined how actively they would use the approach. The ELO strategy does require actively teaching an individual child, potentially interrupting the child's current focus for a short period of time, providing less support as the child learns the skill, and matching the level of support to the child's current proficiency with the skill. Some teachers told us that their philosophy was to treat all the children in the class the same, so focusing on an individual child conflicted with their beliefs about their role as a teacher (Lieber, Capell, et al., 1998). When using ELO, we found that discussions to resolve potential conflicts in philosophy or teachers' beliefs should occur to ensure "buy-in" by the teachers. Further, all of the teachers talked about having times in which they felt "cognitive overload" (i.e., too much to manage; too much to do). Our evaluation supports the belief that ELO can be effective.

IMPLICATIONS FOR PRACTICE

In returning to Buttermilk Station Head Start, we can see the implementation of the range of strategies, including curriculum modifications and embedded learning opportunities, as they occur in the daily routines and activities of a classroom. In this Head Start classroom, children participated fully in the daily curriculum. The teachers often provided additional or more directive verbal support to a child. For example, the teacher gave Cameron step-by-step instructions about how to form the lines to write the number "3" after he identified three ducks in a picture book and wanted to note this in his journal. Modifications also included using concrete physical actions to demonstrate concepts. For example, during center time there was a general class rule that only four children could participate in any center at one time. When Eric wandered into the science center, Ms. Catherine came over to the group and asked Eric to count the number of children. They walked around the small area and counted together out loud. When he counted four, she said, "And you make five. So can you come in here right now?" Eric shook his head and happily moved to another center. At other times the Buttermilk Station teachers used gentle physical guidance to redirect children or assist them in completing a task. On one occasion, Sam stood up and wandered away from the group circle. Ms. Mildred quietly walked over, still singing the "Lady Bug Picnic" song and gently guided him, as they sang and swayed to the rhythm, back to the group.

Modifications were made for Benny's physical limitations. In addition to the "Benny helper," simple adaptations included taping his papers down so they did not slide away, cutting finger foods into smaller pieces, using a cup with a lid to reduce spilling, bringing materials or having children bring materials to him, and moving furniture in the class so that for certain activities he could crawl from one area to another independently.

Embedding specific IEP objectives also happened regularly. Benny, for example, needed to have his limbs, particularly his legs, moved actively in their full ranges to prevent him from getting stiff. Ms. Mildred often sat behind him during one of the group circle times and "put him through" the movements as he participated in the song, rhyme, or choral responding of the moment. Frequently, the movements were part of the current motions being performed by all the children. For example, all the children "peddled" their legs during part of the "ABC" song.

Eric's IEP team had determined that he needed to work on improving his eye–hand coordination; specifically, the IEP stated that he needed to learn to stack at least a three-block high tower of small blocks. In addition to the block area, the teachers noted that they could set up opportunities for Eric to practice this skill in a variety of activities and classroom areas. They had Eric stack the tape cassette boxes after opening circle, the "cubby books" in the reading center, and the forks and spoons on the silverware tray of the snack center.

Cameron needed to work on expanding his verbal communication. The speech therapist was working with him on using a minimum of three-word utterances that had an agent, action, and object (e.g., boy throws ball). The teachers were able to find multiple opportunities in which they could require this response from Cameron. For example, during morning breakfast, before pouring his juice, they would ask, "What do you want?" If he replied, "juice," which he frequently did, they would model the expanded request, "Say, I want juice." This same strategy was used across activities, including art (to obtain needed materials), center time in moving from center to center and obtaining materials out of reach or other kinds of assistance, and on the playground to be pushed on the swings.

A high-quality early childhood program is the necessary foundation for successful preschool inclusion. To be truly successful, however, the program must ensure that the learning needs of young children with disabilities are addressed. High-quality inclusion means that opportunities for a child to meet the goals and objectives stated on the IEP occur during the ongoing routines and activities of the preschool program. Individualizing a child's program, however, requires considerable effort and support. Children with disabilities must have opportunities to participate as fully as typically developing children across all activities and routines. Teachers ensure the child's access to the preschool curriculum by making appropriate adaptations and modifications. Preschool teachers also must know how to embed individualized instruction into the ongoing activities and routines. High-quality individualized instruction within high-quality programs are the teacher's means to ensuring that young children with disabilities make progress.

REFERENCES

Bailey, D. B., McWilliam, R. A., Buysse, V., & Wesley, P. W. (1998). Inclusion in the context of competing values in early childhood education. *Early Childhood Research Quarterly, 13,* 27–48.

Bricker, D., & Cripe, J. J. (1992). *An activity-based approach to early intervention.* Baltimore, MD: Brookes.

Bricker, D., & Pretti-Fronczak, K. (1998). *Treatment validity of the assessment, evaluation, and programming system test for three to six years.* Unpublished manuscript, University of Oregon, Eugene, OR.

Bricker, D., Pretti-Fronczak, K., & McComas, N. R. (1998). *An activity-based approach to early intervention* (2nd ed.). Baltimore, MD: Brookes.

Carta, J. J., Schwartz, I. S., Atwater, J. B., & McConnell, S. R. (1991). Developmentally appropriate practice: Appraising its usefulness for young children with disabilities. *Topics in Early Childhood Special Education, 11,* 1–20.

Davis, M. D., Kilgo, J. L., & Gamel-McCormick, M. (1998). *Young children with special needs.* Boston: Allyn & Bacon.

Fox, L., & Hanline, M. F. (1993). A preliminary evaluation of learning within developmentally appropriate early childhood settings. *Topics in Early Childhood Special Education, 13,* 308–327.

Goodman, J. F., & Bond, L. (1993). The individualized education program: A retrospective critique. *The Journal of Special Education, 26,* 408–422.

Horn, E., Lieber, J., Li, S., Sandall, S., & Schwartz, I. (2000). Supporting young children's IEP goals in inclusive settings through embedded learning opportunities. *Topics in Early Childhood Special Education, 20,* 208–223.

Janko, S., Schwartz, I., Sandall, S., Anderson, K., & Cottam, C. (1997). Beyond microsystems: Unanticipated lessons about the meaning of inclusion. *Topics in Early Childhood Special Education, 17,* 286–306.

Lieber, J., Beckman, P. J., Hanson, M. J., Janko, S., Marquart, J. M., Horn, E., & Odom, S. L. (1997). The impact of changing roles on relationships between professionals in inclusive programs for young children. *Early Education and Development, 8,* 67–82.

Lieber, J., Capell, K., Sandall, S. R., Wolfberg, P., Horn, E., & Beckman, P. J. (1998). Inclusive preschool programs: Teachers' beliefs and practices. *Early Childhood Research Quarterly, 13,* 87–105.

Lieber, J., Schwartz, I., Sandall, S., Horn, E., & Wolery, R. (1999). Curricular considerations for young children in inclusive settings. In C. Seefeldt (Ed.), *The early childhood curriculum: Current findings in theory and practice* (3rd ed.; pp. 243–265). New York: Teachers College Press.

McCormick, L., & Feeney, S. (1995). Modifying and expanding activities for children with disabilities. *Young Children, 50*(4), 10–17.

Mudd, J. M., & Wolery, M. (1987). Training Head Start teachers to use incidental teaching. *Journal of the Division for Early Childhood, 11,* 124–133.

Noonan, M. J., & McCormick, L. (1995). "Mission impossible"? Developing meaningful IEPs for children in inclusive preschool settings. *The Frontline, 2*(1), 1–3.

Notari-Syverson, A., & Schuster, S. (1995). Putting real-life skills into IEP/IFSPs for infants and young children. *Teaching Exceptional Children, 27*(2), 29–32.

Peck, C. A., Killen, C. C., & Baumgart, D. (1989). Increasing implementation of special education instruction in mainstream preschools: Direct and generalized effects of nondirective consultation. *Journal of Applied Behavior Analysis, 22,* 197–210.

Sandall, S. R., Joseph, G., Chou, H., Schwartz, I. S., Horn, E., Lieber, J., Odom, S. L., & Wolery, R. (in press). Talking to practitioners: Focus group report on curriculum modifications in inclusive preschool classrooms. *Journal of Early Intervention.*

Sandall, S., Schwartz, I., Joseph, G., Chou, H. Y., Horn, E., Lieber, J., Odom, S., Wolery, R. A., & ECRII (in press). *Building blocks for successful early childhood programs: Strategies for including all children.* Baltimore, MD: Brookes.

Venn, M. L., & Wolery, M. (1992). Increasing day care staff members' interactions during caregiving routines. *Journal of Early Intervention, 16,* 304–319.

Venn, M. L., Wolery, M., Werts, M. G., Morris, A., DeCesare, L. D., & Cuffs, M. S. (1993). Embedding instruction in art activities to teach preschoolers with disabilities to imitate their peers. *Early Childhood Research Quarterly, 8,* 277–294.

Wolery, M., & Bredekamp, S. (1994). Developmentally appropriate practice and young children with disabilities: Contextual issues in the discussion. *Journal of Early Intervention, 18,* 331–341.

Wolery, M., Martin, C. G., Schroeder, C., Huffman, K., Venn, M. L., Holcombe, A., Brookfield, H., & Fleming, L. A. (1994). Employment of educators in preschool mainstreaming: A survey of general educators. *Journal of Early Intervention, 18,* 64–77.

Wolery, M., & Wilbers, J. (Eds.). (1994). *Including children with special needs in early childhood programs.* Washington, DC: National Association for the Education of Young Children.

CHAPTER 5

Social Relationships of Children with Disabilities and Their Peers in Inclusive Preschool Classrooms

Samuel L. Odom, Craig Zercher, Jules Marquart,
Shouming Li, Susan R. Sandall, & Pamela Wolfberg

KEVIN WAS AN AFRICAN AMERICAN CHILD with Down syndrome enrolled in the Wesley Child Care Center, an urban child care center operated by a church in the community. This classroom is part of the VIP program described in Appendix B. The bustling, colorful classroom contained 15–18 four-year-olds on any given day, and Kevin was the only child with an identifiable disability. When we first observed him, Kevin had learned the schedule and routine of the class and participated in class activities. He communicated using a few words that were hard for others to understand, but he seemed to understand most of the directions from the teacher. Kevin had a clear interest in his classmates. He would watch them at play, smile when they played with him, and try to be a part of their play activities. However, when he tried to play with other children, he often did not appear to know what to do. His peers sometimes saw his attempts to play with them as disruptive. He might take one of the toys with which they were playing, enter a game they were playing without their permission, or accidentally knock down the block tower they had just built. From our viewpoint, Kevin's play was not aggressive or malicious; he would smile and appear friendly. Because he could not communicate well, he could not tell his classmates that he just wanted to play. Our peer-rating assessment and observations told us that in this class Kevin was socially rejected by most of his classmates.

A major advantage of inclusive preschool classes is that children with disabilities are together in the same classroom with typically developing peers. For many years, leaders in the field have told us that a major benefit for children with disabilities is that they will learn social and play skills by observing, interacting with, and playing with typically developing children (Guralnick, 1990; Strain, 1990). Yet, the most well-documented finding in the research literature on preschool inclusion has been that typically developing children do not interact with children with disabilities (in inclusive classrooms or play groups) as often as they interact with typically developing peers (Guralnick, 1999).

If we look only at number or percentage of interactions reported for a group of children, there are two reasons why we may be missing part of the picture of social relationships (particularly social acceptance and rejection) in inclusive programs. First, the assessment of social relationships may extend beyond just collecting information about interactions (although this should be a part of the assessment). It also should involve information gathered from parents, teachers, and even peers. We have called this a multimethod assessment approach, because it uses several different methods and looks at agreement across different sources of information (McConnell & Odom, 1999). Second, when group averages are presented, often a large percentage of children (maybe half) fall below the average and another large percentage are above the average (if there is a normal distribution). Given that such a range exists, it is possible that some typically developing children interact frequently with some children with disabilities (i.e., those that are accepted) and infrequently with others (i.e., those that are rejected). In past research, there has been little study of the social acceptance of children with disabilities in inclusive classes. Also, few studies have used a multimethod approach to assess the social rejection of children with disabilities.

In our research we were very much interested in learning more about social acceptance and rejection of children in inclusive settings. In our ecological systems study, described in Appendix A, we studied the social acceptance and rejection of children across all 16 programs and then we took a closer look at social inclusion at the classroom level. Also, in another set of studies, we learned about the types of teaching strategies that teachers could use to support social relationships of children, and we also learned about factors in the class and program that make such strategies more or less effective.

SOCIAL ACCEPTANCE AND REJECTION IN PRESCHOOL PROGRAMS

In our ecological systems study we collected information about children's interactions with peers, the peers' rating of how much they liked to play with other children in the class, and the teachers' and parents' descriptions of the friendships that children had developed. As described in Appendix A, this information was collected for 80 children with disabilities and 32 typically developing children. Using this information, we developed indexes for identifying children with disabilities who were socially accepted and socially rejected. We describe this methodology in detail in a separate report (Odom, Zercher, Li, Marquart, & Sandall, 2001).

Similar to the research of others, we found, using a multimethod approach, that a about one-third of the children with disabilities in our study (22 out of 80) were socially rejected by their peers. Other researchers have estimated that social rejection occurs in about 10% of the population of typically developing children, and in fact, in our study only one child who was typically developing was socially rejected, according to our measures. Our conclusion is that rejection appears to occur at a higher percentage for children with disabilities. However, we also found that a substantial number of children with disabilities, again about one-third (22 out of 80), were well accepted by their peer group, according to our criteria. This message of social acceptance of children with disabilities in inclusive settings does not often appear in the professional literature, yet it is one that teachers should understand. The next step in this study was to look at the characteristics of children with disabilities who were socially accepted and socially rejected by their peer group.

Social Acceptance

In our research, social acceptance occurred when peers, on the average, rated a child as someone they liked to play with a lot or a little bit, the child played positively with other children and did not play negatively, and the teachers and parents reported that the child had at least one reciprocal friendship (a friendship in which the child with disabilities appeared to select a peer as a friend and the peer selected the child with disabilities as a friend). Case summaries of individual children told us that children with disabilities who were socially accepted by their peers had some common characteristics (see Figure 5.1). Children who were socially accepted had effective social skills, close friendships, could communicate their ideas to others, were affectionate with others, engaged in pretend play, understood class rules, were interested in peer interaction, and appeared to understand the actions of others. These characteristics related to children's skills, behaviors, and presence of a social relationship. For some children with substantial disabilities, the activities they select and their physical characteristics may be associated with social acceptance.

A small number of socially accepted children who were limited by their disability routinely engaged in activities that brought them into playful contact with others (the "play-social routine" theme). For example, Kelly, the child with blindness whom we described in Chapter 1, often would sit in a wagon during outdoor play time because she did not feel comfortable walking around the playground full of energetic, running children and vehicles. On most days, another child would sit in the wagon with Kelly and another child often would pull the wagon. This "wagon time" allowed Kelly to be close to her peers and set the occasion for Kelly to talk with her peers about what they were doing and where they were going.

A characteristic associated with social acceptance that we did not necessarily see as positive was called "perceived dependence." Some children with disabilities were smaller than other children in the class or appeared to be "less able." These children sometimes were treated as

1. Social skills: The child uses behaviors in a social context that are effective in accomplishing his/her social goals, are appropriate for the social context, and/or appear to sustain interactions with peers.

2. Close friendships: The child has at least one relationship with a classmate where the two children seek each other out frequently for play and companionship.

3. Displays positive affect: The child frequently smiles, giggles, and/or laughs at appropriate times when interacting with peers.

4. Communication skills: The child uses a mode of language (either verbal or sign) that the peer group understands to convey effectively ideas, wishes, and desires to other children.

5. Pretend play skills: The child symbolically represents events by using one object to stand for another, animates figures or objects, or assumes a symbolic role during play.

6. Interprets other children's behavior accurately and responds appropriately: The child understands the intent of other children's actions and responds appropriately.

7. Perceived dependence: The child appears substantially less mature or less physically capable than other children, and peers may treat the child like a baby, frequently offering assistance or protection.

8. Expresses affection physically: The child spontaneously hugs, puts arms around, and/or holds hands with peers.

9. Follows class rules and routines: The child obeys the rules of the class.

10. Imitation: The child repeats the motoric or verbal behavior of other children.

11. Easygoing—personable: The child's behavioral style is positive, adaptable, and pleasant.

12. Play/social routines that maximize the opportunity for social interaction with peers: The child engages repeatedly in a specific play activity, area, or equipment that brings him/her into contact with peers and sets the occasions for positive social interaction to occur.

13. Tuned into social interaction: The child interacts with other children infrequently but observes and appears interested in peers' social activities.

14. Peer entry: The child successfully gains access to ongoing peer play situations, often by watching at the periphery and then engaging in the same actions as the children involved.

Figure 5.1. Social acceptance themes ordered from the most frequent to the least frequent number of children associated with each.

"little sisters or brothers," with the typically developing children (and sometimes the teachers) providing more assistance than they really needed. For example, Marnie, a preschooler with cerebral palsy, was nonambulatory but of normal intelligence and had good upper body motor control. Except for getting in and out of her wheelchair, Marnie was a very capable little girl, taking care of herself quite well in a competitive toy conflict that might arise. However, the children (and teachers) in the classroom appeared to think of her as more dependent than she actually was and provided considerable assistance. The teachers even called her their "china doll."

Social Rejection and Themes

Children identified as socially rejected (ranked in the bottom three children in their class on the peer-rating measure) on the average were rated by peers as children they did not want to play with, sometimes engaged in substantially less positive interaction or substantially more negative interaction with peers than other children, and had no or few reciprocal friendships reported by parents or teachers. Again, our case summaries revealed that children who were socially rejected shared some similar characteristics (see Figure 5.2).

Some children who were socially rejected lacked the skills necessary for making friends. Not being able to communicate effectively with peers, interact in a positive and sustained way, and play (especially pretend play) with peers were all associated with social rejection and occurred for many children. For example, the description of Kevin, at the beginning of this chapter, reflects a child lacking the skills to engage in successful social interactions with peers.

Some children identified as socially rejected were disruptive in class, had conflicts with peers, and were physically aggressive toward peers. For these children, being negative toward their classmates was more of a problem than not having skills they needed to engage in positive interactions.

Another smaller group of children who were socially rejected tended to withdraw from social interaction or preferred adult interaction to playing with peers. For example, Jimmy was a child with autism enrolled in a community-based child care program. When children attempted to play with him, he would ignore them. Sometimes they would try to help him line up to go outside, and he would reluctantly allow himself to be pulled to the line (by a peer). When peers were close to him, he sometimes would move away.

1. Speech/language/communication problems: The child does not effectively convey his/her thoughts, ideas, or social goals to others.

2. Conflict with peers: Child commits actions to which another child objects.

3. Lacks social skills: The child does not have or use the necessary social skills for engaging other children in positive social interactions.

4. Disruptive in class: The child does not follow teacher directions, does not participate in classroom routines, and/or engages in tantrums or protests when teachers attempt to direct the child's activities.

5. Socially isolated or withdrawn: The child actively withdraws from or avoids interactions with peers.

6. Physically aggressive toward peers: The child hits, pushes, shouts at, or speaks negatively to peers in the class.

7. Lacks play skills: The child does not have the necessary symbolic play skills to participate in playful activities with peers in the classroom.

8. Prefers adult interactions: The child chooses to talk or play exclusively with adults.

Figure 5.2. Social rejection themes ordered from the most frequent to the least frequent number of children associated with each.

INCLUSION IN AND EXCLUSION FROM THE PEER CULTURE

Our work on social acceptance and rejection of children with disabilities gave us insight into the social relationships occurring in inclusive settings. A next step in our research was to gain a closer view of children's experiences in the classroom. In classrooms, preschool children develop a shared set of meanings and values about the social behavior of their peers. They use these shared meanings in their play and routine social interactions with classmates. Pamela Wolfberg and others on our research staff (Wolfberg et al., 1999) have described this as *peer culture*, and our "closer look" at the social dimensions of preschool inclusion has led us to try to understand how children with disabilities become part of, or are apart from, the peer social culture of the classroom. To do this, we examined closely the observations and information we collected for 10 children located in six classrooms in California and Maryland. We chose these children for this study because they represented a cross-section of the large sample described previously and also because they all had "significant disabilities" (e.g., autism or pervasive developmental disorder; profound hearing impairment; mental retardation; significant emotional disturbance). Our methodology and data analysis are described in detail in Wolfberg and colleagues (1999).

A first important finding was that all the children, even those identified as accepted and rejected in the previous study, showed a desire to participate in the peer culture, were included by peers in classroom activities, and also, at times, experienced exclusion or rejection by peers.

Desire to Participate

Because many of the children we observed in this study did not have typical communication, social, or play skills, they sometimes expressed their desire to participate in ways that were different from typically developing children. Rather than engaging directly in play with classmates, some children might watch, follow, or imitate peers during play time. This awareness of and interest in others might increase as a result of being in the inclusive program. For example, one mother told us:

> Like before, when I [took] him to a playground, you know there would be kids running all around and it was just like he didn't even notice they were there. But now, I notice he watches them and, you know, tries to follow what they are doing and everything. (Wolfberg et al., 1999, p. 75)

The desire of children with communication skills to participate in the peer culture was more traditional. They shared, gestured, talked with, and even wrote about peers. Children with other disabilities indicated their desire to participate in other ways, such as taking roles in play. For example, Tammy, a child described as having severe emotional disturbance, had a particular interest in playing the role of a dog. "Tammy's classmate, Wolfy, pretended to feed two baby dolls with a plastic bottle. Tammy crawls over to Wolfy and takes the dolls in her mouth, growling and shaking her head from side to side" (Wolfberg et al., 1999, p. 76).

Inclusion in the Peer Culture

Peers included children with disabilities in the peer culture in different ways. This inclusion often occurred when the peers and the children with disabilities had established a common ground. That is, they had interests in common that served as a basis for social play and communication. For example, Jorge, a child with autism, and his classmates had an interest in the movie, *The Lion King*. This common theme and songs from the movie allowed Jorge to enter "Lion King" activities in which his classmates were involved (Wolfberg et al., 1999). Also, peers sometimes responded sensitively to the less conspicuous or subtle social attempts made by the children with disabilities, and sometimes they "transformed" the unfamiliar or unconventional behavior into a normal part of the peer culture. Again, using her interest in playing the dog character, Tammy one day joined a group of boys in the block area.

> They build a structure around her, enclosing her on all sides. Tammy pretends she is a dog, crawling on all fours, barking and growling, eventually knocking down the structure. The boys yell, "The dog broke the cage." Tammy runs away on all fours—the boys scream and run after her. (Wolfberg et al., 1999, p. 77)

Peers also provided help, guidance, and care for some of the children with disabilities. As noted above, sometimes this care was a result of the peer's perceived dependence of the other child and at other times it was spontaneously given. Jackie, a child with developmental delays, who often resisted social approaches from peers, sometimes would receive help in classroom activities. "Teacher Maggie demonstrated how to make a ball of Play Doh. Jackie makes a passable ball and says 'ball.' A peer, Deanna, takes Jackie's ball, smoothes it out, and hands it back to Jackie" (Wolfberg et al., 1999, p. 78).

Exclusion from the Peer Culture

As well as being included in the peer culture, at times children with disabilities were excluded. Sometimes such exclusion occurred through apathy and indifference; peers might treat the children with disabilities as if they were invisible.

> Angelia goes to the pretend play area as her peers engage in table activities. She stands in the middle and leans on the table, waiting. She looks around, apparently, for someone to join her. She continues to watch and wait, remaining all alone in the play area. (Wolfberg et al., 1999, p. 79)

At other times, exclusion from the peer culture resulted from children misunderstanding the unconventional behavior of classmates with disabilities or overlooking their social attempts. Gary, a child with ADD/ PDD, sometimes approached a play activity with his own perspective or play theme guiding his actions, did not take into account a peer's perspective or play theme, and was sometimes "out of synch" in blending his play with others'. This made it hard for peers to understand Gary's play and, at times, led to his not being incorporated into the play activity.

A clear value in this peer culture, as in any other culture, is the rules followed in using space and materials. Sometimes conflicts developed between children with and without disabilities over property. "Jackie tries to grab the animals in the center of the table. Matthew grabs them from her, places his body over them, and tries to return them to the table. Jackie pushes Matt and makes an angry noise" (Wolfberg et al., 1999, p. 80).

At times, such conflicts result from a misinterpretation of the actions of others by the children with disabilities, leading to their own exclusion. Cathy, a child with developmental delays, is working on a puzzle.

> A boy, Andrew, sits nearby. Cathy is having trouble placing a piece, commenting, "That no work." When Andrew tries to help, Cathy protests, "No! No!" and slaps his hand. A little later, he reaches over and tries to place a piece in Cathy's puzzle. She scowls at him and hits him again. (Wolfberg et al., 1999, p. 80)

Such behavior sometimes would result in "tattling" to the teacher. For example, peers in Kevin's (the child with Down syndrome described previously) classroom were very aware of his behavior. More than with any other child in the classroom, classmates would report to the teacher when he violated the cultural values of the peer group or the classroom rules. Rarely could we spend a morning in the class without hearing reports from peers to the teacher about Kevin's misbehavior.

Summary

Our view of social acceptance and rejection from the "10,000-foot level" tells us that young children with disabilities enrolled in inclusive settings are at high risk for social rejection by peers, but that not all children are socially rejected and a sizable percentage of children appear to be well accepted. When we viewed children's inclusion in and exclusion from the peer culture in classrooms from the "ground level," we found that all children (even those who are socially rejected) at times are included in the peer culture. However, those children experience exclusion from the peer culture as well, with rejected children experiencing this exclusion more than children who are socially accepted (Wolfberg et al., 1999).

The characteristics we found associated with social rejection and exclusion could be seen as "red flags" for teachers. For children who lack the communicative, social, and play skills to engage in positive interactions with peers; children who often are in conflict with peers and are disruptive; and children who withdraw from social contact with peers, teachers should look for ways they can help these children become more socially engaged in the classroom. Development of social and play skills as well as inclusion in the peer culture are important goals for these children. Several teaching strategies for promoting social engagement are described in the next section of this chapter.

SUPPORTING CHILDREN'S SOCIAL COMPETENCE, SOCIAL RELATIONSHIPS, AND INCLUSION IN THE PEER CULTURE

Clearly, rejection by peers in classroom settings is a barrier to successful inclusion for preschool children with disabilities. In our research, we studied different types of teaching approaches that might lead to greater participation of children with disabilities in the peer culture, as a way of promoting the social competence of children with disabilities. In doing this, we followed a conceptual framework that organized teaching strategies according to level of intensity—by which we meant the amount of time and "special education training" required of the classroom teacher (Brown, Odom, & Conroy, in press; Odom & Brown, 1993). This framework is presented in Figure 5.3, and each strategy is discussed below.

Classroom-wide Interventions

One group of intervention approaches involves setting up the classroom so that children with disabilities have the opportunity to interact with socially responsive peers. A second approach is designed to affect the attitudes of children in early childhood classrooms toward peers with disabilities.

Developmentally appropriate practices and inclusion in early childhood programs with socially responsive peers. When involved in a setting with typically developing peers, some children with disabilities become part of the group. They suggest ideas, pretend play, share materials, and do the other things needed to become part of the peer culture. For these children, simply placing them in developmentally appropriate preschool settings with a socially responsive peer group is sufficient to support their acceptance and active participation in the peer culture. As we discussed earlier, other children need more support, and for them more-individualized approaches may be necessary.

Affective interventions to influence attitudes. Affective intervention approaches nurture children's positive attitudes toward peers who have disabilities. The NAEYC antibias curriculum has the intent of promoting

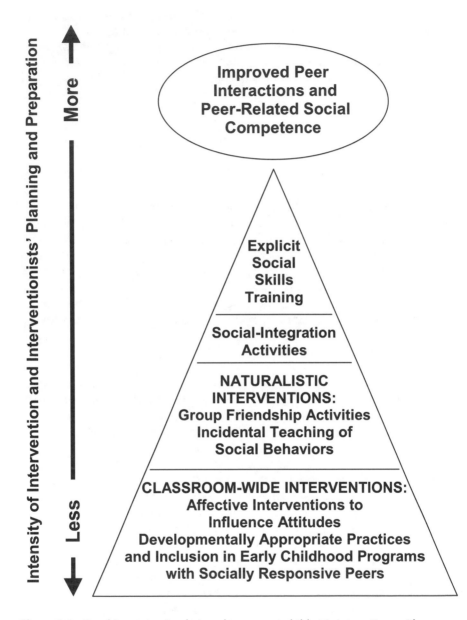

Figure 5.3. Teaching strategies designed to support children's interactions with peers, ordered by time required for implementation and expertise of the teacher. *Note.* Reprinted with permission from "An Intervention Hierarchy for Promoting Preschool Children's Peer Interactions in Naturalistic Environments," by W. H. Brown, S. L. Odom, and M. A. Conroy, in press, *Topics in Early Childhood Special Education.*

positive attitudes toward individuals from diverse cultures and with diverse abilities, although the recommendations tend to be fairly broad and have not been validated by research. In a direct approach to fostering positive attitudes, Favazza and Odom (1997) developed a multicomponent teaching approach that involves a story time, with books about individuals with disabilities; a guided discussion; and play activities involving children with and without disabilities. Such an approach has a powerful impact on children's attitudes.

Naturalistic Interventions

The research of others, and our own work, has examined approaches that are now grouped under the general description of "naturalistic teaching" (Rule, Losardo, Dinnebeil, Kaiser, & Rowland, 1998). The common features of these approaches are:

1. They occur in the child's natural settings (for example, play activities occurring in the classroom).
2. The teacher identifies times during the day when a child has the opportunity to engage in specific social skills (or participate in the peer culture).
3. The teacher organizes the activity so the opportunity occurs and provides the support necessary.
4. The natural consequences of participating in the learning opportunity are fun and rewarding for the child (for most children, playing with and being accepted by their peers are very rewarding).

Incidental teaching of social behaviors. Incidental teaching is one form of naturalistic intervention. Teachers arrange the opportunity for children to become involved in social interaction with a peer (e.g., place him/her close to another child at a play activity), wait for the child with disabilities to show interest in the other child's play or the materials the other child is using, and if necessary provide a demonstration of how the child could play with others or suggest ways the child could play (Brown et al., in press). Other strategies similar to this are called enhanced milieu training, pivotal response training, and embedded learning opportunities (discussed in Chapter 4).

Group friendship activities. This teaching approach has a long history and much research showing that it can be used by teachers and is effective for some children (McEvoy et al., 1988; Twardosz, Nordquist, Simon, & Botkin, 1983). In group friendship activities, the teacher builds in an affection or prosocial component to songs, finger-plays, and/or games children play in the classroom. (In Simon Says, instead of the teacher saying, "Simon Says take a giant step," she might say, "Simon Says give _____ a hug.") The activities happen in a small or large group that the teacher leads, so they might be part of the opening circle time or a special activity during the day. Also, the children with disabilities who are socially rejected are the focus of positive attention from peers. In our research (Frea, Craig-Unkefer, Odom, & Williams, 1999), we have used songs and games such as:

> Do you know the apple man?
> London Bridge
> Simon Says
> Can you do what I do?
> If you are happy and you know it?
> Have you every met a wiggly worm?
> Hokey Pokey

Consider this example: Arin was involved in the group friendship activities. He was a 4-year-old African American boy in our study described as having a developmental language disorder with echolalia. He tried to play with other children, but his attempts were largely inappropriate. Peers in the classroom either ignored his attempts to play, moved away from him, or told him to go away. As the teacher began using the group friendship activities, Arin's positive interactions with his peers increased in both the group activities themselves and also in play activities occurring at other times of the day. This change may have happened because peers developed a different impression or attitude toward Arin as a result of spending time in positive, fun, and affectionate activities with him—which was quite different from what happened before.

Social-Integration Activities

Another teaching approach that we studied was social-integration groups (Frea et al., 1999; Odom & Choi, 1998). In social-integration activities, the teacher brings together a small group of children for a specific play activity. The teacher selects two or three peers in the class who are good communicators and players and one or two children who are socially rejected. She organizes an activity in a specific part of the room in which only these children will play for a 5–10-minute period. In our research, these activities have included: dress-up, Mr. Potato Head, cooking and eating, birthday party, doctor, dough shapes, drawing, puzzles, block house and people, housekeeping, and dinosaurs/animals. The teacher introduces the activities, suggests play roles, and also suggests ideas for playing with "your friends." However, the teacher does not take a play role and gradually removes herself from the activity. At the end of the play period, sometimes signified by the ringing of a kitchen timer, the children may continue to play in the activity or move on to another.

Lou was a 4-year-old African American girl who was socially rejected by her peers. She was both physically and verbally aggressive toward her peers, which limited the amount of time she spent in positive play activities (because they would avoid her). During the morning "centers time" in her classroom, Ms. Moran, Lou's teacher, brought together several of her peers and Lou in the social-integration play activity. She suggested ways in which the children could play together (taking turns, saying the names of other classmates, using a nice voice), introduced the activity ("We are going to make dinner with our friends today"), and described ways children could play with each other in the activities (ways to make dinner with your friend). She also provided some suggestions after the children began playing. When Lou became involved in these social-integration activities, her positive play increased and her negative interaction decreased. These changes also were seen in other play activities occurring later in the day, in which the teacher did not provide an introduction or suggestions. For Lou, the chance to play with peers in a positive way, which was supported by the teacher, led to changes in the amount of time spent and quality of her behavior with peers (Frea et al., 1999).

Explicit Social Skills Training

We view social skills training as the most intensive teaching level because it requires the most time and training for the teacher and child. Social skills training may involve only the children with disabilities, it may involve only the typically developing peers in the classroom (to teach them ways they can promote the social play of the children with disabilities), or it may involve both. Teachers follow planned lessons in which they first describe a specific skill to be learned (e.g., sharing), demonstrate the skill with another child (share a toy with another child), and have children practice the skill while other children in the group watch to see whether the child actually did the skill (share with another child in the group). Usually right after the small-group lesson, the children are involved in a social-integration activity in which they practice the skill that was introduced and discussed in the lesson. The teacher, at first, gives frequent prompts or suggestions, but then reduces the prompts. When only the peers are involved in the training, this approach has been called "peer-mediated" teaching (Odom, Chandler, Ostrosky, McConnell, & Reaney, 1992) or "peer buddies" (English, Goldstein, Schafer, & Kaczmarek, 1997). When children with disabilities are involved, this approach has been called "child-specific" interventions, and when both are involved, it is called a "comprehensive" intervention. Recent research suggests that the peer-mediated approach may be the most effective of these approaches, especially when the children with disabilities have limited communication, social, and play skills (Odom et al., 1999). In our research, we have found that the effectiveness of this teaching approach also depended on how well the teachers implemented the intervention (Odom, Wolery, & Choi, 1998). Teachers who have worked with us and used the strategies have reported the long-term effectiveness of this approach with some children.

Practical Considerations and an Example

In our studies, we have found that not all interventions are effective with all children. For example, in our research with Arin and Lou, each child was involved in one other teaching approach; for Lou the social-integration activities were more effective than the group friendship activities, and the reverse was true for Arin (Frea et al., 1999). Also, we found that it may be possible and even important for teachers to try different teaching approaches with different children and even to combine approaches. The story of Jason and Sydney provides an example (Odom & Choi, 1998).

Jason was a 5-year-old boy with communication and motor delays; Sydney was the same age but was diagnosed as having autism, and they were both socially rejected by peers in the classroom. Jason was a little clumsy and played with others in a rather intrusive way. Whenever he tried to enter a play activity, he would be disruptive and peers would tell him to go away. Sydney, who could communicate in sentences although he had some echolalia, would choose activities in which other peers were not playing, would tell peers to go away if they tried to play, and was sometimes disruptive in the classroom. For these two children, the teachers decided to use the social-integration activity approach during their centers time.

Jason was the first child involved in the social-integration activities. The teacher chose two peers (Harold and Mary) and one other child with disabilities to be involved in the activities. At the beginning of centers time, right after circle, all the children in the class selected an activity, except for Jason and his group, who were assigned to the social-integration activity, which changed every day. At first, the teacher provided suggestions for the children, but after a while she found that was not necessary because the children were playing well together. In fact, the teacher commented that she was concerned that she was not doing her job of teaching because she was monitoring rather than interacting with the children. In the social-integration activities, Jason's positive play with others increased dramatically, and he developed a friendship with Harold. They would choose to play together, sit together, and talk with each other in other activities during the day. As a result, the number and quality of Jason's interactions increased in other activities as well.

After Jason's interactions had begun to change, the teacher started working with Sydney. However, Sydney was very resistant to coming to the social-integration activity. He would complain and occasionally have a tantrum because he had to leave his play activity. Changing from one activity to another was an issue for Sydney. The teachers decided to try a different approach in which they combined a naturalistic teaching strategy with a peer buddies approach. The teacher first talked with three different peers about how they could get Jason to play with them, how they needed to try another way if what they tried first did not work, and how they needed to be persistent. When Sydney became involved in an activity during centers time, one of the peer buddies would start to play with him in "his" chosen activity. This play could occur for a 5-minute period, and then the peer could go play elsewhere. Different peers played with Sydney each day. During these play sessions, Sydney's positive social play increased markedly. He would allow others to play with him, he would use the peers' names, he would watch the peers when they were playing in other activities, and occasionally he would attempt to join other activities in which they were playing. However, this teaching approach lasted for only 2 weeks before the school year ended. During other times of the day, Sydney continued to play alone. We think this was because the teaching strategy was used for only a short time. To see more "generalized" gains for Sydney, he needed support for a longer period of time.

IMPLICATIONS FOR PRACTICE

From our research on children's social interactions and social relationships, there are several clear implications for teachers.

- Some children with disabilities in inclusive (and probably noninclusive settings as well) are at risk for social rejection from peers, while others are well accepted. Teachers should look for "red flag" characteristics of children that are associated with social rejection.

These are (1) lack of communication, social, and play skills necessary for being a "good player"; (2) aggressive or disruptive behavior that alienates other children; and (3) social isolation or withdrawal.

- Teaching approaches exist for promoting the social interactions of children with disabilities. These approaches range in time and previous training required of the teacher. The teacher might begin by using a less intensive approach, such as arranging the environment or naturalistic teaching, and move to a more intensive approach if the child does not become more involved in successful social interactions.
- Different teaching approaches work differently for different children. The teacher should choose an approach that fits the characteristics of a child or even modify and combine approaches based on the child and the classroom context.
- For most children who are socially rejected, an emphasis on promoting positive interaction with peers, involving single or multiple teaching approaches, probably will have to occur over a long period of time. Short-term interventions lasting only 2–4 weeks may not be long enough to produce the enduring changes needed for children.
- Ensuring that children with disabilities are involved in positive social interactions and play with peers across the day (rather than just during a teaching or intervention time) is important. Pairing a naturalistic teaching strategy with more-intensive approaches would be important for children who are socially rejected.
- For children with problem behavior (aggression, disruptive behavior), utilizing a system of positive behavior supports (Sugai et al., in press) to reduce the problem behavior while also using one of the teaching strategies described in this chapter to increase positive social interaction with peers may be necessary.

Above all, teachers should keep in mind that for any of these approaches to be successful, they have to be *fun* for the children with disabilities and their peers.

REFERENCES

Brown, W. H., Odom, S. L., & Conroy, M. A. (in press). An intervention hierarchy for promoting preschool children's peer interactions in naturalistic environments. *Topics in Early Childhood Special Education*.

English, K., Goldstein, H., Schafer, K., & Kaczmarek, L. (1997). Promoting interactions among preschoolers with and without disabilities: Effects of a buddy skills-training program. *Exceptional Children, 63*, 229–243.

Favazza, P. C., & Odom, S. L. (1997). Promoting positive attitudes of kindergarten-age children toward individuals with disabilities. *Exceptional Children, 63,* 405–418.

Frea, W., Craig-Unkefer, L., Odom, S. L., & Williams, D. (1999). Differential effects of structured social integration and group friendship activities for promoting social interaction with peers. *Journal of Early Intervention, 22,* 230–242.

Guralnick, M. J. (1990). Social competence and early intervention. *Journal of Early Intervention, 14,* 3–14.

Guralnick, M. J. (1999). The nature and meaning of social integration for young children with mild developmental delays in inclusive settings. *Journal of Early Intervention, 22,* 70–86.

McConnell, S. R., & Odom, S. L. (1999). Performance-based assessment of social competence for young children with disabilities: Development and initial evaluation of a multimethod model. *Topics in Early Childhood Special Education, 19,* 67–74.

McEvoy, M. A., Nordquist, V. M., Twardosz, S., Heckaman, K., Wehby, J. H., & Denny, R. K. (1988). Promoting autistic children's peer interaction in an integrated early childhood setting using affection activities. *Journal of Applied Behavior Analysis, 21,* 193–200.

Odom, S. L., & Brown, W. H. (1993). Social interaction skills interventions for young children with disabilities in integrated settings. In C. Peck, S. Odom, & D. Bricker (Eds.), *Integrating young children with disabilities into community programs: Ecological perspectives on research and implementation* (pp. 39–64). Baltimore, MD: Brookes.

Odom, S. L., Chandler, L. K., Ostrosky, M., McConnell, S. R., & Reaney, S. (1992). Fading teacher prompts for peer-initiation interventions for young children with disabilities. *Journal of Applied Behavior Analysis, 25,* 307–318.

Odom, S. L., & Choi, Y. (1998, December). *Specialized interventions for promoting inclusion of children with disabilities.* Paper presented at symposium entitled Inclusion Stories: Current Findings of the Early Childhood Research Institute on Inclusion at the DEC International Conference on Children with Special Needs, Chicago.

Odom, S. L., McConnell, S. R., McEvoy, M. A., Peterson, C., Ostrosky, M., Chandler, L. K., Spicuzza, R. J., Skellenger, A., Creighton, M., & Favazza, P. (1999). Relative effects of interventions supporting the social competence of young children with disabilities. *Topics in Early Childhood Special Education, 19,* 75–91.

Odom, S. L., Wolery, R., & Choi, Y. (1998). *Selection and use of social interaction teaching by teachers in inclusive preschool programs.* Unpublished study.

Odom, S. L., Zercher, C., Li, S., Marquart, J., & Sandall, S. (2001). *Social relationships of preschool children with disabilities.* Manuscript submitted for publication.

Rule, S., Losardo, A., Dinnebeil, L., Kaiser, A., & Rowland, C. (1998). Translating research on naturalistic instruction into practice. *Journal of Early Intervention, 21,* 283–293.

Strain, P. (1990). LRE for preschool children with handicaps: What we know, what we should be doing. *Journal of Early Intervention, 14,* 291–296.

Sugai, G., Horner, R. H., Dunlap, G., Lewis, T. J., Nelson, C. M., Scott, T., Liaupsin,

C., Reuf, M., Sailor, W., Turnbull, A. P., Turnbull, R. H., & Wickham, D. (in press). Applying positive behavior support and functional behavior assessment in schools. *Journal of Positive Behavior Interventions.*

Twardosz, S., Nordquist, V. M., Simon, R., & Botkin, D. (1983). The effects of group affection activities on the interaction of socially isolated children. *Analysis and Intervention in Developmental Disabilities, 3,* 311–338.

Wolfberg, P. J., Zercher, C., Lieber, J., Capell, K., Matias, S. G., Hanson, M. J., & Odom, S. L. (1999). "Can I play with you?": Peer culture in inclusive preschool programs. *Journal of the Association for Persons with Severe Disabilities, 24,* 69–84.

CHAPTER 6

Collaborative Relationships Among Adults in Inclusive Preschool Programs

Joan Lieber, Ruth A. Wolery, Eva Horn,
Jennifer Tschantz, Paula J. Beckman, & Marci J. Hanson

JIMMY WAS DIAGNOSED WITH AUTISM when he was 2½. He had very little expressive language and showed a number of stereotypic behaviors, including rocking and finger flicking. Jimmy initially received early intervention services in a center-based program for toddlers with developmental delays. At 3, he began preschool in a private special education program, where he was able to follow simple directions and participate in classroom activities. When that program closed and his family requested public school services, they learned that their school system was piloting a program to include preschoolers with disabilities in community-based child care programs. Jimmy's family saw this program as an excellent opportunity.

As part of this pilot program, the school system promoted a collaborative team model for the families and professionals involved in the inclusion programs. According to one service provider, "The whole attitude that the preschool [special education] office is trying to put forth . . . is the collaborative model. . . . None of us has any magic. It's in our collective work that we can get things done" (Lieber, Beckman, & Horn, 1999, p. 7).

When children with disabilities are included in preschool programs, teamwork becomes a necessity. No matter what type of individualized-service model a program uses, early childhood special education (ECSE) teachers, early childhood education (ECE) teachers, related service professionals, administrators, and families must work together to meet the needs of individual children. Teamwork requires adults to make somewhat different adjustments, depending on the program model used. For example, when special educators are itinerant teachers who provide direct service or consultation to early education teachers, as in Jimmy's program, the special educators have to adjust to not having their own classrooms. Also, they must adapt to the working styles of different early education teachers and must effectively convey information about the needs of individual children (Horn & Sandall, 2000). Early education teachers have adaptations to make as well. They must be willing to have a special educator spend time in their classrooms and make time available to talk with her or him about the children with disabilities in their class.

Special educators and early childhood educators in a team teaching model have somewhat different adjustments to make. In this model, teachers who were used to operating independently now have to share instructional responsibilities. The teachers must work out a mutually acceptable teaching approach and agree on ways to meet children's learning needs.

The importance of adults working as a team for successful inclusion became one of the major themes of our ecological systems study. We generated this theme from interviews with teachers and administrators, and from our observations of adults interacting in the classroom, as well as during team meetings when no children were present. From these data we identified seven factors that were facilitators for effective collaboration among adults in inclusive programs (Lieber et al., 1997; Lieber, Beckman, & Horn, 1999).

Of course, even in inclusive programs, there are barriers that prevent adults from working together effectively. So we designed a research study to help teams consisting of administrators, teachers, other professionals, and sometimes family members to use a problem-solving approach to improve their collaboration. The approach consisted of three steps. In the first step team members identified their goals for inclusion. In the second step they identified the barriers preventing the team from reaching the goals. Finally, teams planned ways of overcoming those barriers. Teams in Maryland, Tennessee, and Washington used this problem-solving approach. As they did, we observed and participated in team meetings, observed team members in the classroom, and interviewed them about their perceptions. We were interested in whether participating teams became more collaborative, and whether there were changes in their inclusive programs as a result.

In this chapter, we first identify the seven factors that help adults develop positive professional relationships in inclusive programs. Our focus is on relationships among professionals; we consider parent/professional relationships in Chapter 7. Next we describe a collaborative problem-solving approach that one team of teachers used and report the changes that took place in the relationships among teachers and other professionals and in program policies.

FACTORS FOR EFFECTIVE COLLABORATION

Joint Participation in Program Development

For many of our programs, inclusion was a new experience, and often the impetus began with program directors or administrators (Lieber et al., 2000). However, it was left to the staff members to figure out what their program ultimately would become. We found that when staff members contributed to their program's development, inclusion was facilitated.

Staff members who jointly planned and shared the responsibility of running the program had a sense of ownership and commitment to making inclusion work. As one principal said, "The inclusion experiences that have been really positive have been those outgrowths of people who want to work together, are committed to working together, and have gradually increased the time they work together." In contrast, staff members who were not involved in developing or running the program often had a hard time working together.

Shared Philosophy and Instructional Approaches

Sharing a teaching philosophy also contributed to effective working relationships. We found that professionals who had common beliefs about teaching agreed about the goals for their program and how to achieve them. Without those shared beliefs, relationships were stressful. One special educator admitted, "There's been some real bumpy roads. The early education teacher . . . was under the assumption that the children were not going to need much hands-on [help], so I think that hurt a lot in the beginning" (Lieber et al., 1997, p. 72).

Shared "Ownership" of the Children

In each of our programs there were children with and without disabilities, and a third critical factor was whether responsibility for all children was shared by team members. One special educator told us, "When it comes time to write report cards, we work together on that. When it comes time to write IEPs, we work together on that too" (Lieber et al., 1997, p. 72). Sharing responsibility was more of a challenge for programs using an itinerant approach. According to one itinerant teacher, "The biggest barrier is this idea that a lot of teachers have, 'they're your special needs kids, you're only here one day a week for [X] minutes, and you don't understand what we go through on a daily basis' " (Lieber et al., 1997, p. 73).

Communication

The informal and formal communication among staff members also promoted successful professional relationships. In some programs there were planning times that gave staff members time to meet and work collaboratively. Unfortunately, in some programs the time for joint planning was limited.

Communication was also enhanced when staff members took advantage of informal opportunities. Informal contact might occur during lunch or while waiting to meet children as they arrived. One occupational thera-pist relished the chance to be in the classroom with the early education teacher so they could "bounce ideas off each other."

Changing Professional Roles

When we spoke with teachers, a number of issues arose about how their jobs had changed in inclusive programs. We found that teachers who were flexible had good working relationships. In one team teaching class-room, the special educator said, "I'm not just a special educator in our model. I work with all the children."

In other programs, job clarity became a problem. When staff members' responsibilities were unclear or poorly understood, there was dissatisfac-tion in working relationships. In one team teaching classroom, the special educator was unsure about her role with her co-teacher. When a child with a disability was given little assistance during an activity, the special educator commented, "It's hard to see this happen . . . but how much do you do? What is our role, are we mother or boss?" (Lieber et al., 1997, p. 75).

Stability in Relationships

Familiarity among the adults often had a positive impact on relationships. In one program, stability in the town's population increased familiarity among staff members. According to the director of special education:

> Our staff has been very stable. All these people get to know each other because they stay here. So when something like inclusion comes along, we have a built-in and positive atmosphere and a high level of cooperation among people. (Lieber et al., 1997, p. 76)

Administrative Support

Administrative support also contributed to good working relationships among staff members. Administrators provided support by recognizing the contributions of individual participants, allocating resources, allowing time for joint planning, and listening to staff concerns.

IMPLEMENTING A MODEL FOR COLLABORATION

In this section we describe how staff members used a problem-solving approach to increase their inclusive activities at the Winwood Early Childhood Center. The collaborative team that used this model developed it through the initiative of two teachers who participated with us in the ecological systems study. When other staff members in the program noticed our work with these teachers, they expressed an interest in increasing their time in inclusion. So we formed a collaborative team to identify goals for inclusion and the barriers to meeting those goals. Then the team developed and implemented a plan to overcome the barriers.

Winwood, a public early childhood center with 149 staff members, served 700 children from birth through age 8. There were seven different programs at the center, including Healthy Start and Even Start (federally funded programs for mothers and their children), programs for infants and toddlers, preschoolers, and primary-aged children with disabilities; Head Start; and state-funded prekindergarten programs.

Winwood served children from a diverse community, and the principal, Lydia, saw her program as an integral part of the community. Families whose children attended Winwood consistently gave glowing reports about the center's programs. One mother noted, "What impressed me is the love they have for the children. I just haven't seen it at any other school."

The principal called Winwood's approach to inclusion a "buddy-class" model. She paired a class of preschool children with disabilities with a Head Start or prekindergarten class. The classes were located near each other to allow for integrated activities. The teachers were free to bring their classes together for as much or as little time as they wished, although the principal expected that they would do some activities with their buddy class. So the model of individualized services these teachers used was an integrative-activities model, although some teachers engaged in team teaching.

A Buddy-Class Pair of Teachers

One of the buddy-class pairs, Sandy and Jane, had participated in the ecological systems study. Sandy, an ECSE teacher, and Jane, a Head Start teacher, had classrooms across the hall from each other. When we first worked with them, their classes participated in integrative activities for 30 minutes a day, 4 days a week. But a year after we came to Winwood, the principal asked Sandy and Jane to make a change in their classes so that a majority of their students would be dually enrolled in Head Start and special education. That combination was consistent with the federal policy requiring that at least 10% of the children in each Head Start program have disabilities, as well as a local Head Start initiative to increase that number to 20% of Head Start enrollment. The teachers used the principal's request as an opportunity to extend their collaborative efforts.

Although the initiative to dually enroll children came from the administration, Sandy and Jane jumped at the opportunity. In Sandy's words, dual enrollment "opened the door for us to do more." The change meant that the buddy classes were together for most of the day. As Sandy described it, "We consider it more team teaching. Pretty much all of our day is together now. We are eating meals together, free-play time is together, language activities are also integrated. It's a big difference."

Shared philosophy. At the beginning, Jane's and Sandy's philosophies on teaching were quite different. Sandy noted, "Jane is more child-directed. [I] lead more than [I] let the children lead." When Sandy and Jane engaged in more team teaching, Sandy also began changing her instructional approach. Reflecting on this shift, Sandy commented, "My teaching style has definitely changed over the year." When we asked Sandy why she made the change, she replied, "I realized how beneficial it was for the children. I saw that the children really needed it, so I need to change my style. I looked at Jane's classroom and her work time. I saw what was going on and I thought, 'That's what I want.' "

Shared ownership of the children. When the children and teachers began spending more time together, there was some loosening in individual ownership of the children. Sandy described one discussion she had with Jane about this change.

> We talked the other day, and I said, "Let's trade kids during circle." And Jane said, "Well, I really like to have just my kids." And I said, "You know what? We're the only ones that know they're *our* kids. The children don't know now . . . and if we don't put any point to it, they'll never know." And Jane said, "No, I guess you're right. But I want to be able to see what they're doing." I said, "Well, I see that, and I'll share with you."

Communication. Being together so much of the day affected the teachers' working relationship. As Jane explained, it gave them the opportunity to exchange information more often and to engage in more informal communication. "We talk every day, several times a day, and of course, we're together part of the day. We start our morning waiting for the buses together. We have breakfast together. So we talk at that time besides meetings that we have together." Not only did they talk frequently but Sandy and Jane were quite comfortable in their communication. Their strong communication links extended to the classroom assistants as well. As Sandy said, "I think we all feel that we can talk to each other and say,

'Hey that went well,' or 'Hey it didn't go well for me, what can we do to work that out?' "

Joint planning. When Sandy and Jane began working together, their limited time together made joint planning a low priority. When their time commitment changed, joint planning became more of a necessity. To focus their planning efforts, the teachers used a summary of skills needed by the children, as prepared by the prekindergarten coordinator, and they incorporated the children's missing skills into their lessons.

Expansion of Collaboration

The principal named Sandy and Jane as one of her strongest buddy class pairs. Unfortunately, collaboration among other early education and special education teachers was limited. To capitalize on the relationships that did exist, we began to work with all the teachers on a team model to promote collaboration among the staff members and inclusion opportunities for the children. Our partnership lasted for 2 years.

The core members of the team were early childhood education and early childhood special education teachers who met monthly as a large group. Other participants met with the team intermittently and included related service providers (e.g., motor specialists, speech pathologists) and the principal. During the second year of the partnership, classroom assistants joined the team.

Team-Identified Barriers and Solutions for Year One

Goal. During the first year of our partnership, we met 10 times as a group. Since most of the team members expressed an interest in doing "more inclusion," that became our goal for the first year.

Barriers to meeting the goal. Over the year, team members identified barriers that prevented them from spending more time in inclusive activities. Two of those barriers were logistical: buddy classes that were not located near each other, and buddy-class teachers with incompatible schedules.

Other barriers were administrative. Special education, Head Start, and the prekindergarten program all had different regulations that affected inclusion. Also one day a week children with disabilities did not attend class so that their teachers could conduct district-wide special education assessment. The disconnect between the programs was emphasized when monthly meetings were held separately for ECSE preschool teachers and ECE teachers. Teachers were also concerned because they had no time for joint planning.

Overcoming the barriers. The team spent 5 of their 10 meetings planning and implementing strategies to overcome the barriers they identified. They agreed that many of the barriers needed administrative intervention, so three of the five meetings included the principal and/or the director of the prekindergarten program for the school district.

As a result of the meetings, the principal made administrative changes for the next school year. She made sure that one hour per week was set aside for joint planning time for buddy-class teachers. Classrooms for the buddy-class partners were moved so that they were close to each other, and meetings of the preschool ECSE and ECE teachers were held on the same day to facilitate meeting jointly. Other administrative changes were serendipitous. A district-level assessment team was created, so the ECSE teachers no longer were needed to do eligibility assessments. Since the children with disabilities now attended classes 5 half-days a week, there were more opportunities for inclusion.

Teachers also made changes so that when the next school year started, they'd be ready to spend more time in inclusive activities. They chose a buddy-class partner at the end of the year and presented their decision to the principal. Those partners then jointly constructed their class schedules for greater compatibility. In other initiatives, two team members contacted each of the occupational therapists and physical therapists to inquire about their willingness to provide related services in the classroom rather than serving children on a pull-out basis.

Team-Identified Barriers and Solutions for Year Two

Goal. Because the second year began with the logistical changes in place, the team was ready to identify another goal. In interviews, team members decided to focus on learning how to provide instruction that emphasized the objectives for individual children and on using data to see whether the children had met their objectives.

Barriers to meeting the goal. For most teachers, the primary barrier was a lack of information and experience. For example, one of the Head Start teachers said that she had difficulty coming up with objectives for the children with whom she worked. She said she might be able to identify a specific skill a child needed, but was not sure about the skills that should be taught before or after. Other teachers said they were not sure when they would have time for data collection.

Overcoming the barriers. During five of the eight meetings of the team, members generated ideas and shared solutions to meet their goal. One of the leaders of the group, Sandy, presented a child's IEP objective in the fine motor domain: to copy + and 0. She said, "How can we work on this objective throughout choice time, rather than just having the child sit down and practice the shapes?" Using the different areas of the room (e.g., art area, dramatic play area), the teachers brainstormed materials and activities that would develop those fine motor skills. The teachers decided they could put lots of writing tools in the art area. And they decided they could set up the dramatic play area as a restaurant, and if the child was a waiter, he or she could practice writing by taking meal orders.

During another meeting, an ECSE teacher gave an example of embedding an objective for one of the prekindergarten children: identifying colors. She said during an art activity she had the crayons visible but out-of-reach. When Richard wanted a crayon, he needed to tell her the color he wanted, and then she'd hand it to him. The teacher also had other children hand Richard crayons he requested, giving them chances to practice their color recognition too.

Teachers also shared ideas about data-collection strategies and forms they had developed to collect data. One of the ECSE teachers made a form with icons representing each of the activity centers. Under each icon was room to list specific children's objectives that might be met in that center. There was also space on the form to record, with tallies or anecdotally, children's progress on the objectives.

Teachers also came up with ideas about how to find time for data collection. For example, one buddy-class team (two teachers and two assistants) planned a cooking activity following a trip to the grocery store. They decided to split the class into two groups, using one adult to facilitate the activity and one adult to collect data on the children's objectives.

Although teachers planned for their classes at other times, the large-group team meeting was a valuable resource. Teachers benefited from the rich source of ideas. For example, one ECSE teacher asked the group for help with Stevie, a child with disabilities who had difficulty participating during a large-group music activity. Three teachers offered ideas, like letting Stevie pass out instruments to the other children.

Changes in Relationships and Policies

Using information and themes from our ecological systems study as a guide, we documented the changes in the collaborative relationships over the 2 years of our partnership with the Winwood staff members, as well as the changes in school policies.

Joint participation in program development. Teachers at Winwood showed a strong investment in developing a more inclusive program during both years of our project. Teachers consistently participated in the large-group meetings, and individual buddy-class teams were eager to meet with us to discuss barriers they encountered in their particular classrooms. Over the course of the 2 years, teachers spent more time in inclusive activities and more time planning for those activities during the buddy-class planning time.

When programs begin inclusion, it is vital for participants to take the initiative in fostering program activities. At Winwood, team members met with the principal to suggest ways to facilitate inclusion. The most significant evidence of staff members taking the initiative, however, took place after our partnership ended. During the following school year, a leadership team consisting of three ECSE teachers, a prekindergarten teacher, and a motor specialist became facilitators of the large-group meetings. The leadership team developed the agenda for each meeting based on the interests of the other participants, recorded the events of the meeting, and communicated decisions of the team to the administration. The team wrote a report with recommendations for the principal about how inclusion could continue to grow at Winwood.

Shared philosophy and instructional approaches. During the first year, we spent two group meetings on a discussion of teachers' philosophies and instructional approaches. These discussions and teachers' observations of their partners' teaching during inclusive activities led to a convergence in approach for several teachers. One special education teacher said she got "a better understanding of the prekindergarten program" and that she wanted to "try something different." Another special education teacher said, "My teaching style has definitely changed over the year. I have been able to set up my classroom during play time and utilize it more as a child-directed setting."

Communication. Communication between teachers also improved over the course of the project. The opportunity to communicate increased when teachers spent more time in inclusive activities. One Head Start teacher reported, "We see each other so much during the day that we can change our plans in the middle of the morning."

The planning time that teachers instituted during the second year gave them more opportunity to communicate and time to plan instruction. According to one teacher, "Maggie might say, 'I have the need for my kids to have more practice on this skill,' and then we would come up with activities that would incorporate it." Additional time to communicate allowed one buddy-class team to "write out a monthly play time map and to list children's goals for each center in the classroom." Sharing a philosophy and communicating were critical relationship factors for successful buddy-class partnerships.

Relationships among buddy-class partners. Three partnerships continued and thrived during our 2 years at Winwood. One partnership, established during the second year, was not as successful. Lila, the ECSE teacher, and Marion, the prekindergarten teacher, identified their problems with inclusion as problems with their relationship. According to Marion, problems occurred because "we weren't always on the same curriculum . . . I never felt we were on the same commitment level . . . I felt I was the leader and there wasn't any initiative coming [from my partner]." Similar concerns were expressed by Lila, who said, "We didn't find an agreement on how to do [inclusion] . . . I don't think she liked working with me . . . I felt like I had to conform to the way that Marion thought."

Stability in adult relationships often has a positive impact on collaboration, and stability increased over our 2 years at Winwood. During the first year, the principal chose the buddy-class teams, and two of the ECSE teachers were paired with different partners in the morning and afternoon sessions. During the second year, most teachers chose their own partners, and each was paired with the same partner for both morning and afternoon sessions. Teachers' preferences were respected, and having only one partner facilitated instructional planning.

Although there were substantial changes in relationships among teachers, other factors remained unchanged. One of those factors was shared ownership of the children.

Shared "ownership" of the children. In successful inclusion programs, responsibility for children is shared jointly by ECE and ECSE professionals. At Winwood, children continued to be described as "mine or hers." For example, a Head Start teacher speaking to her children said, "It's circle time, go to your own room." That separation was fostered by administrative requirements that were different for ECSE and ECE programs. One Head Start teacher told us, "I think we're each responsible for certain kids . . . because at the end of the day I have an extra half hour more [with the kids than the ECSE teacher] does so I'm responsible for getting my notes to my children and getting their wraps together and so forth." So although the program at Winwood had many factors that typically contribute to successful inclusive programs, shared ownership of children continued to be a barrier.

Administrative support. Administrative support was manifest in a number of ways at Winwood. Although the consensus among the teachers was that the building principal provided substantial support to individual teachers and to the team, they felt that support was lacking for more sweeping change. In a follow-up interview with the leadership team, members expressed a need to ask the principal to clarify how inclusion operates at Winwood. Additionally, in spite of the principal's support, many team members felt there was less support from other agencies. The relationship with Head Start was a particular problem and did little to facilitate inclusion. One Head Start teacher said, "I have seen little support from [Head Start]. I don't know if they're even concerned about what we're doing. They just don't respond. At the beginning of the year there were administrators saying, 'You can't do it this way.' Now they don't even come out, period."

Summary

We have described one of the sites where a team implemented a problem-solving model to provide more inclusive opportunities for children. We worked with the teachers to identify and develop strategies to overcome the barriers at one early childhood center. The team worked together for 2 school years and identified unique barriers to inclusion in each of the 2 years.

During the first year, the teachers identified and then worked with the administration to overcome logistical barriers. Those barriers, related to the coordination of class schedules and the schedules of related service providers, as well as time for planning, were significant. Before teachers could tackle the next set of barriers, the first set needed to be eliminated, and they largely were with the support of the administration. During the second year, teachers primarily considered instructional barriers. They used each other as resources to explore solutions to concerns about specific students, how to target the IEP objectives of children with disabilities during less-structured activities, and how to document children's progress.

As team members tackled the barriers to inclusion at Winwood, we noticed changes in factors that facilitate successful inclusion. Greater numbers of buddy-class teachers contributed to program development and teachers improved in their communication and in understanding others' instructional philosophies. Winwood's administration supported teachers' attempts to change their practice. There were some factors, specifically, sharing "ownership of the children," and support from outside agencies, that proved more resistant to change.

IMPLICATIONS FOR PRACTICE

Our work and that of others (McWilliam, 1996; Peck, Furman, & Helmstetter, 1993) suggest that it is critical for professionals who provide inclusive services for children to develop collaborative working relationships. This process is ongoing, and it evolves and changes over time. Below, we list a number of recommendations suggested by staff members and families from the programs we have worked with. Some of the ideas can be used by teaching staff and others who work directly with children; other ideas apply to administrators who shape the programs themselves.

Recommendations for Teachers

Have a positive attitude toward change. In our experience, the teams that were successful in working together were those that were open and willing to try something new. When Sandy and Jane had the opportunity to work together more closely for the benefit of all their children, they saw it as a chance to "grow and stretch."

Take the initiative. It's not sufficient for adults who are working together to be willing to change. Teachers need to take the initiative to make that change happen. Although administrators often take the lead in program development, teachers can play leadership roles as well. For example, teachers at Winwood organized group meetings to discuss inclusion, developed questionnaires to plan partnerships for the following school year, and met with the principal to share their views on scheduling issues.

Be flexible. Of all the exhortations we've heard from teachers, "be flexible" is the one we have heard most often. Flexibility is crucial when groups of adults work together, because change and compromise are necessities. At the beginning of the school year at Winwood, ECE teachers and ECSE teachers developed their class schedules independently. Yet when the children began to spend more time in inclusive activities, each teacher willingly altered her schedule to accommodate their increased time together.

Develop communication strategies. The teachers we worked with developed a number of effective communication strategies. In programs that use an itinerant-consultation model to provide individualized services, adults may have limited face-to-face contact. In those programs, notebooks prove to be very useful. Notebooks also have worked in many programs where families are unable to see their child's teachers every day.

In contrast, in the programs in which staff members are in daily contact, informal communication plays a larger role. Staff members can share information over lunch, out on the playground, and after the children leave for the day.

But with either of these strategies, teachers still need to set aside time for planning. In one of our community-based child care programs, ECE teachers, itinerant ECSE teachers, related service providers, and family members met monthly during children's nap times to plan for specific children. The teachers at Winwood felt the need so acutely that they asked the principal to set aside time before school each Friday when no other meetings would be scheduled so they could focus their efforts on joint planning.

Recommendations for Administrators

As program leaders, administrators play a large part in ensuring that team members with different backgrounds, personalities, and expertise work together to improve children's outcomes. We have some specific recommendations for administrators who want their staff members to work as a collaborative team (Wolery & Odom, 2000).

Support a shared philosophy. Collaborative teams in inclusive programs plan and implement interventions to enhance children's learning. Every inclusive program should have a written philosophy that supports the concept of enhancing outcomes for children. A written statement, particularly one that team members have contributed to, helps the team to function optimally. Developing a shared philosophy is not an easy task. There are significant differences in instructional beliefs among families, early childhood educators, and special educators. Even when individuals use the same words, they may be talking about different concepts. Because such differences are inevitable, they need to be discussed openly.

Support adequate meeting times. The issue of having adequate time for meetings is a chronic and pervasive problem. The larger the team, the more difficult it is to schedule meetings. If a team is small, possible meeting times are before or after school or during nap time. With larger teams, it is sometimes necessary for an administrator to provide release time for participants who are responsible for working with children.

Support working toward a common goal. Teams may have a variety of goals, including discussing objectives for individual children or objectives for the program, but before any meeting that the team holds, an agenda should be developed. A variety of forms already exist to help teams construct an agenda (Friend & Cook, 1996; Thousand & Villa, 1992), and they all include the goals for the meeting, a place to list progress toward meeting the goals, and a structure for assigning tasks to team members.

Support team members' sharing their expertise. Effective team collaboration requires team members to share their expertise across disciplines. This is necessary for teams to work together effectively. Sharing of expertise requires team members to be both teachers and learners. Often professionals provide training to another team member, who will then deliver the service. Administrators can facilitate the sharing of expertise to ensure that the expectations of roles and responsibilities are defined and understood by all team members.

Support team members' use of collaborative skills. It is evident that team members are using collaborative skills when together they plan and implement an inclusive program that enhances outcomes for children. As team members make programming recommendations, however, logistical difficulties and philosophical differences may arise. When this occurs, the team's facilitator should be prepared to guide the team through problem-solving techniques.

The team facilitator can work with the team to

Identify the problem
Brainstorm solutions, list ideas, defer judgment
Identify the most promising solutions or combinations of solutions and judge them against the problem
Select a solution
Devise a step-by-step action plan to carry out the solution

Support team members' sharing the work. Although the entire collaborative team may participate in planning, the roles of individual team members may vary. Children's programs are almost always carried out by an ECE teacher or a co-teaching team. Other team members may be family members or may participate regularly as itinerant specialists. Whatever the level of involvement, team members should be available to answer questions and offer new ideas. Likewise, team members who serve in an indirect capacity should visit the preschool program occasionally to show their commitment to the child and the team. Administrators can support this process by ensuring that all team members understand their roles and know what others expect from them. Often, an administrator's push, praise, and availability is all that it takes to ensure that team members share in the work necessary to sustain a successful inclusive program.

REFERENCES

Friend, M., & Cook, L. (1996). *Interactions: Collaboration skills for professionals.* White Plains, NY: Longman.

Horn, E., & Sandall, S. (2000). The visiting teacher: A model of inclusive ECSE service delivery. Natural environments and inclusion [Monograph Series No. 2]. *Young Exceptional Children*, pp. 49–58.

Lieber, J., Beckman, P. J., Hanson, M. J., Janko, S., Marquart, J. M., Horn, E., & Odom, S. L. (1997). The impact of changing roles on relationships between professionals in inclusive programs for young children. *Early Education and Development*, 8(1), 67–82.

Lieber, J., Beckman, P. J., & Horn, E. (1999). Working together to provide services for young children with disabilities: Lessons from inclusive preschool programs. In S. Graham & K. R. Harris (Eds.), *Teachers working together: Enhancing the performance of students with special needs* (pp. 1–29). Cambridge, MA: Brookline Books.

Lieber, J., Hanson, M. J., Beckman, P. J., Odom, S. L., Sandall, S. R., Schwartz, I.S., Horn, E., & Wolery, R. (2000). Key influences on the initiation and implementation of inclusive preschool programs. *Exceptional Children*, 67(1), 83–98.

McWilliam, R. A. (1996). How to provide integrated therapy. In R. A. McWilliam (Ed.), *Rethinking pull-out services in early intervention: A professional resource* (pp. 147–184). Baltimore, MD: Brookes.

Peck, C., Furman, G., & Helmstetter, E. (1993). Integrated early childhood program. Research on the implementation of change in organizational contexts. In C. Peck, S. Odom, & D. Bricker (Eds.), *Integrating young children with disabilities into community programs: Ecological perspectives on research and implementation* (pp. 187–206). Baltimore, MD: Brookes.

Thousand, J. S., & Villa, R. A. (1992). Collaborative teams: A powerful tool in school restructuring. In R. A. Villa, J. S. Thousand, W. Stainback, & S. B. Stainback (Eds.), *Restructuring for caring and effective education: An administrative guide to creating heterogeneous schools* (pp. 73–108). Baltimore, MD: Brookes.

Wolery, R. A., & Odom, S. L. (2000). *An administrator's guide to preschool inclusion*. Chapel Hill: University of North Carolina, Frank Porter Graham Child Development Center and the Early Childhood Research Institute on Inclusion.

CHAPTER 7

Family Perceptions of Inclusion

Paula J. Beckman, Marci J. Hanson, & Eva Horn

WHEN TONY'S TEACHER RECOMMENDED that he be placed in an inclusive preschool program, his mother, Karin, had mixed feelings. She liked the idea that he would be around typically developing peers who might be good models for his language development. And she had heard that the program that was being recommended was very high quality. But, Tony had been premature, and had been participating in a home-based infant program for the past 18 months due to some developmental delays. Karin liked the home-based teacher and thought that Tony benefited from the one-to-one attention he received. His infant teacher gave her many ideas about things she could do with Tony, and Karin liked being so involved. She wanted Tony to "catch up," so that he would be ready for kindergarten when the time came, and she was not convinced that he would get enough attention to his individual needs in an inclusive classroom. Many of her concerns were based on the previous experience of her niece—who had been placed in an inclusive program in third grade, but who had received little special attention. Another worry was that the preschool Tony would attend was not in her neighborhood. He would have to ride the bus for nearly 45 minutes, and it would be difficult for her to talk to the teachers and visit the program on a regular basis.

In recent years, services for young children with disabilities have been greatly influenced by two major movements in early childhood special education: the trend toward delivering services in a manner that is family-centered, and the trend toward inclusion and participation in natural environments (Beckman et al., in press; Strain, Smith, & McWilliam, 1996; Turbiville, Turnbull, Garland, & Lee, 1996; Vincent & McLean, 1996). As a result of these converging influences, it has become increasingly important to understand how families view the preschool programs in which their children participate as well as how they view inclusion. In general, the literature suggests that families view inclusion positively, although they express many common reservations (Erwin, Soodak, Winton, & Turnbull, 2001). However, there is little in the literature that explains what factors influence family perceptions of inclusion. Thus, investigators participating in the Early Childhood Research Institute on

Inclusion were interested in learning what influenced family perceptions of the inclusive programs in which their children participated. This was consistent with ECRII's overall conceptual framework, which emphasized the importance of learning about inclusion from many different perspectives (see Chapter 1).

We carried out five studies focused on families, including the ecological systems study, the family survey, the follow-along study, the transition study, and the community study. In all of these studies, family members told us, in extensive, open-ended interviews, about the experiences that they and their children had in inclusive preschool programs.

In the ecological systems study, we obtained family perceptions about children's inclusive preschool programs from 80 families of children with disabilities and 32 families of children without disabilities (Beckman et al., in press; Beckman et al., 1998; Hanson et al., 1998). We also followed 33 of these families for the remaining 4 years of our project, continuing to interview them about inclusion and checking on their children's progress (Hanson et al., in press b). In another study of 22 families, we focused on transitions from early intervention programs to public school preschool programs and learned about how families and service providers make decisions about placing children in inclusive and segregated special education preschool classes (Hanson et al., in press a). We observed planning meetings, reviewed documents, and interviewed primary caregivers, service coordinators, and providers from the sending programs. In a further study, we extended our analysis of facilitators of and barriers to inclusion to a wider array of families ($n = 354$). Finally, in a study of families' and children's involvement in the community, we talked with focus groups of families and community providers to learn about factors that influenced children's participation in community settings.

THEMES RELATED TO FAMILY PERCEPTIONS

The description of Tony illustrates the many factors that influence parents' perspectives about inclusion. Although the focus and the methodology of the ECRII studies varied, we found that six major themes emerged repeatedly across the studies. In this chapter, we will describe these six themes and discuss their implications for practice.

Overall Program Quality

In interviews, family members told us repeatedly that their perceptions of inclusion were based on their overall perceptions of the quality of the program (Beckman et al., in press). Although the availability of inclusive opportunities was important to many families, it could not make up for more general concerns about the overall quality of the program. Parents' perceptions of quality could be grouped into two general areas. The first had to do with how they felt their child was doing in the program. When parents believed that their child was happy in the program and was making progress, they tended to express satisfaction with the program. The second major way parents judged the program was based on the specific characteristics of the teacher and the quality of the parents' relationship with the teacher.

The role of inclusion in families' judgments about the quality of programs varied. For some families, inclusion was a very important feature of the program, whereas other families did not know whether the program in which their child was placed was inclusive. However, when families judged the overall quality of the program as poor or had reservations about the teacher, the fact that the program was inclusive was not enough to override these problems. As one father shared: "It's something we all know. It doesn't matter how wonderful the school is. If you have a lousy teacher, it doesn't matter."

Frame of Reference

Family perceptions of inclusion also were heavily influenced by their individual frame of reference (Beckman et al., in press). By "frame of reference" we mean those things that participants in inclusive settings bring to this experience. The families in the ECRII studies had many different values and perspectives. One of the most important was their view of how their child's disability might influence his or her participation in the program. This perception varied greatly from family to family and often had little to do with severity of disability. For example, one mother whose daughter had relatively mild motor delays was skeptical about her daughter's participation in an inclusive kindergarten program. She noted:

> "She can't handle the scissors right now . . . so it's things like that with the fine motor skills . . . that would probably keep her from really entering a regular elementary school . . . because those children know how to operate scissors and they can run and keep up and the teacher wouldn't have to take the extra time to hold her hand and walk slower with her . . . academically, I think she can handle it, but physically . . . " (Beckman et al., in press).

Other factors also contributed to families' frames of reference. One such factor was the family's view of the role of preschool. Many families viewed preschool as a place in which children were getting "ready" to participate in elementary school. For these families, participation in specialized programs during preschool did not necessarily imply that their child would be in a special education program during elementary school—indeed, it was often seen as preventing the need for special education in the future. For such families, whether the program was inclusive during preschool, was not as important as the possibility that it would prepare their child to participate in elementary programs.

The goals that parents had for their child were also an important part of their frame of reference (Beckman et al., in press; Hanson et al., 1998). Some family members believed that their children needed opportunities for social interaction with other children or for good language models. These parents often saw inclusive programs as offering the opportunities for learning that special education classrooms lacked. In contrast, other parents felt that their child needed highly specialized, intensive services. When they perceived inclusion as detracting from these goals, they expressed concerns.

Previous experience with the service system was another factor that shaped parents' frames of reference (Beckman et al., in press; Hanson et al., in press b). This was particularly true when families had some previous experience with inclusion. The nature of these experiences frequently had an important impact on their feelings about inclusion. For example, a few of the families we interviewed had older children or relatives who had been part of the special education system and who had participated in inclusive programs. When their previous experiences were positive, they frequently looked forward to the opportunity for inclusion with their young child. However, negative experiences led them to be wary of inclusion and to question some of its basic premises.

Finally, the kinds of options that their children had for social contact at home and in the community also influenced how they saw inclusion in their children's preschool program (Beckman et al., 1998; Beckman et al., in press). For example, some of the families we saw had large extended family and friendship networks that offered many opportunities for social contact with other children. These family members often judged the program in terms of how it addressed such achievements as walking or cognitive development. These families tended to judge the program less on factors related to inclusion and more on the availability of services that would promote the children's needs. Although the development of social skills may have been important to them, they saw their own social networks as the primary source of such opportunities.

Families' frames of reference influenced their view of the program in general, their interactions with professionals in the program, and their views of inclusion. It is also important to note that service providers also bring a particular frame of reference to their work with children and families in inclusive programs. Their frames of reference include their own views about the child and the child's disability, their view of the role of preschool, their perspectives on inclusion and on the role of families, and their previous experiences within their system and with children and families.

The Match Between the Program and Perceived Child and Family Needs

Family members reported good experiences with inclusive programs when the services the programs provided matched their child's needs. In some cases, this match had to do with very specific needs of the child; in others it involved a match with broader family needs. For example, if parents perceived that their child needed a great deal of structure to make progress, they tended to like programs that were highly structured and dislike programs that were less structured.

While the importance of a good match could be seen in a variety of ways, three areas stood out as particularly important: logistical considerations, availability of specialized services, and relative class size. Considerations about logistics frequently centered on the cost and location of the program. For example, when asked why she placed her son in a particular program, one mother said: "I just heard that they had a good learning system there at that school and since it's right near my work, that's why we enrolled him. . . . There wouldn't have been no way I could've worked and gotten over there to get him. That played an important part, that it was close to my job" (Beckman et al., in press).

The availability of specialized services was also important to families. Many parents who had concerns about inclusion focused on a fear that their child would not have access to needed services or the kind of individualized, structured approach that they associated with special education. When parents felt that inclusion implied less focus on their child's individual needs, they expressed concerns. One parent explained: "The parents have fought so hard to get classes that focus on their child's disabilities that to buy into inclusion means that they have to abandon things they have fought for for the last three to five years, and they aren't prepared to do that" (Beckman et al., in press).

Finally, as they contemplated the prospect of inclusion in elementary school, many parents expressed concerns about class size and ratio of adults to children in the classroom. They expressed concerns that their children's needs would get lost when there were many children in the classroom and when there was a large ratio of children to adults.

Limited Choice and Decision Making

One of the major components of a family-centered approach to service provision is the notion that families are the primary decision makers for their child and that they have a right to participate actively in making decisions for their child (Winton, 1993). A consistent finding throughout the studies conducted as part of the ECRII was that parents often felt that they had little choice about their children's placement in inclusive or traditional special education programs (Beckman et al., in press; Hanson et al., in press a; Hanson et al., in press b). Even when school districts offered placement choices, family members usually felt their options were limited. Options were often limited by such factors as school or program regulations, the type of programs that were available, lack of professional training, lack of information about options, and logistical constraints. For example, in one program, inclusive placements were not available for 3-year-olds (even though such placements were available for 4-year-olds) because the school was not directly involved in serving 3-year-olds without disabilities and had not made arrangements to work with local day care centers. Often, parents felt that teachers or administrators had already made the placement decisions before meeting with them and that the parents were simply expected to agree with the decision. In many cases, the options available were extremely limited. One mother said: "I guess the down and out of it was that I didn't have a choice. Well, I did have a choice—either he goes or he doesn't, and that choice wasn't acceptable, having him not go" (Beckman et al., in press). In other instances, options were available, but parents were not informed about the options in a way that allowed them to exercise their choices.

Family choices decreased even more over time. From our follow-along study, we found that the limitations increased as children grew older and entered the elementary school program. Much of the time, family members reported they had no alternative—either professionals had indicated that the child was not "ready" for regular school, or they felt that an inclusive placement was not available. One mother observed:

> "I do want Nina to be in an inclusive classroom. But the thing is there's just not enough schools here in the south end area providing those services. So we have no other alternative but to put her in a self-contained classroom." (Hanson et al., in press a)

Need for Information

Family members' ability to exercise choice was often hampered by limited information about inclusion, their rights, and the program in general. We found that the extent to which families had the information they needed to participate effectively in decision making varied considerably. Some families had a great deal of information and were well informed about their rights and the options available for their children. These families were often able to influence the decision-making process. Others had extremely limited information, about even basic aspects of their children's programs. Family members' frustration at the lack of information was expressed by one mother when she said: "I need somebody to listen to me and talk to me and let me know something about the program, and that's what I need and they haven't told me" (Hanson et al., in press a).

The way in which information was or was not communicated to families was a critical factor in their ability to make decisions. Usually, families simply were given information about the choices that were available in a particular system; alternatives that were not available were never described. Moreover, emphasis often was placed on those services that the program was encouraging. For example, in one program, parents who actively advocated to have their child placed in a local day care center were often granted that option; however, we never observed this alternative being offered to families at the IEP meetings we attended.

Access to information was influenced by many factors, including socioeconomic status, education, culture, and the way in which service providers communicated with them. For example, one custodial grandmother did not have a telephone and could not read. Although she was officially notified about IEP meetings through the mail, she did not always understand what she had received from the school and often did not have anyone available who could read it to her. As a result, even though she had strong opinions about her granddaughter's educational program, she typically missed IEP meetings and had few other opportunities to express her opinions.

Support for Families

Throughout the ECRII studies, the importance of providing support to families whose children were participating in inclusive programs was clear. Very often, we found that it was the efforts of one key individual that made the difference in a child's opportunity to participate in an inclusive program. These individuals came into contact with the families in our studies in a variety of ways—sometimes they were teachers or administrators that the family came to know and trust; other times they were parents of other children. They offered information and support to families in ways that allowed the families to identify and enroll their children in the best programs. They often helped families interpret information or provided access to resources that the families might not have had in other ways. For example, one mother described her service coordinator in glowing terms by saying, "She's given me contact people . . . she's done her job above and beyond the call of duty in my eyes because she was very helpful" (Hanson et al., in press a).

IMPLICATIONS FOR PRACTICE

Our findings have important implications for service providers working in inclusive preschool programs. One implication is that, as they develop inclusive programs for young children, it is important to families that service providers remember the basics—specifically, the importance of a good program and a good relationship with families. Basic aspects of creating a good program are essential to families, regardless of whether the program is inclusive. At a minimum, this includes developing a program that directly addresses the needs of individual children (see Chapter 4). In the emphasis on family-centered service delivery, providers need to remember that one of the most basic needs expressed by most families is that their child receive services that match his or her needs. If parents feel that their children are not benefiting from the program, they are unlikely to be satisfied, even when the program is inclusive. An essential component of a good program is a competent teacher who communicates effectively with families, provides useful information, and builds families' trust.

These findings also highlight the importance of the individual relationships that are formed between service providers and families. In our work, the nature of these relationships had an important influence on the way families felt about their children's program. Additionally, the finding that children's participation in inclusive settings often hinged on the efforts of one key individual highlights the importance of building strong relationships with families. These findings are consistent with the more general literature concerned with families (Beckman, 1996) and suggest that such relationships play an important role in inclusive programs.

As providers develop relationships with families, they frequently learn more about the family's frame of reference. Learning about how the parents view the child and the child's disability, what goals family members have for the child, and what previous experiences family members have had, can help providers understand the family's view of the program. In many cases, such knowledge also can help providers better match the program to the needs of the family.

Finally, it is critical that providers recognize the important link between communication, access to information, and decision making. For families to make well-informed decisions about their child and their child's program, they need access to good information. However, providing real access to information is not simply a matter of delivering a packet of information about the program that has been prepared by school officials. Information must be provided in ways that are consistent with family members' language, culture, experience, and educational background. Providers need to encourage families to ask questions and explore options in order to determine the best match for the needs of the child and the family.

REFERENCES

Beckman, P. J. (Ed.). (1996). *Strategies for working with families of young children with disabilities*. Baltimore, MD: Brookes.

Beckman, P. J., Barnwell, D., Horn, E., Hanson, M. J., Gutierrez, S., & Lieber, J. (1998). Communities, families and inclusion. *Early Childhood Research Quarterly, 13*, 125–150.

Beckman, P. J., Greig, D., Barnwell, D., Hanson, M. J., Horn, E., & Sandall, S. R. (in press). Influences on family perceptions of inclusive preschool programs. *Journal of Early Intervention*.

Erwin, E., Soodak, L., Winton, P., & Turnbull, A. (2001). "I wish it wouldn't all depend on me": A critical analysis of research on families of children with disabilities and inclusive early childhood settings. In M. Guralnick (Ed.), *Early childhood inclusion: Focus on change* (pp. 127–158). Baltimore, MD: Brookes

Hanson, M. J., Beckman, P. J., Horn, E., Marquart, J., Sandall, S. R., Greig, D., & Brennan, E. (in press a). Entering preschool: Family and professional experiences in this transition process. *Journal of Early Intervention*.

Hanson, M. J., Horn, E., Sandall, S., Beckman, P., Morgan, M., Marquart, J., Barnwell, D., & Chou, H-Y (in press b). After preschool inclusion: Children's educational pathways over the early school years. *Exceptional Children*.

Hanson, M. J., Wolfberg, P., Zercher, C., Morgan, M., Gutierrez, S., Barnwell, D., & Beckman, P. J. (1998). The culture of inclusion: Recognizing diversity at multiple levels. *Early Childhood Research Quarterly, 13*, 185–209.

Strain, P. S., Smith, B. J., & McWilliam, R. A. (1996). The widespread adoption of service delivery recommendations: A systems change perspective. In S. L. Odom & M. E. McLean (Eds.), *Early intervention/Early childhood special education: Recommended practices* (pp. 101–124). Austin, TX: Pro-Ed.

Turbiville, V. P., Turnbull, A. P., Garland, C. W., & Lee, I. M. (1996). Development and implementation of IFSPs and IEPs: Opportunities for empowerment. In S. L. Odom & M. E. McLean (Eds.), *Early intervention/Early childhood special education: Recommended practices* (pp. 77–100). Austin, TX: Pro-Ed.

Vincent, L. J., & McLean, M. E. (1996). Family participation. In S. L. Odom & M. E.

McLean (Eds.), *Early intervention/Early childhood special education: Recommended practices* (pp. 59–76). Austin, TX: Pro-Ed.

Winton, P. J. (1993). Providing family support in integrated settings: Research and recommendations. In C. Peck, S. Odom, & D. Bricker (Eds.), *Integrating young children with disabilities into community programs: Ecological perspectives on research and implementation* (pp. 65–80). Baltimore, MD: Brookes.

CHAPTER 8

Community Participation of Children with Disabilities

Paula J. Beckman & Marci J. Hanson

WHEN GAIL AND HER FAMILY moved to a new city, she wanted her daughter Sarah to have a chance to meet other children and become part of their new community. Sarah was 5 years old and had cerebral palsy. Her dream began to come true when she met Angie while struggling to get Sarah into her wheelchair so that they could go into church. Angie stopped, asked if she could help, and then helped Gail maneuver the chair up the short staircase leading to the church. She made it a point to introduce Gail to the director of the Sunday school and initiated a discussion about how to make sure that it was a good experience for Sarah. It was the beginning of a friendship that would become a major source of support for Gail and Sarah. Gail invited Angie's daughter, Kelsie, to their house for a play date, which quickly became a regular event. In the summer, they frequently met at the neighborhood pool, so that the girls could have an outing together. As the women got to know each other, Angie decided to petition the church board to build a wheelchair ramp.

Most literature concerned with the inclusion of young children has focused on two major contexts: school classrooms and day care settings. However, there has been growing recognition that inclusion involves the participation of children with disabilities in a *broad array of contexts* within their communities (e.g., neighborhoods, religious organizations, and recreation centers), as well as an emphasis on the importance of building social linkages for individuals with disabilities (Amado, 1993; Beckman et al., 1998; Turnbull, Turnbull, & Blue-Banning, 1994; Wellman & Leighton, 1979). This is consistent with literature focused on older persons with disabilities, in which community-based services have long been advocated (Moon, 1994). It is also consistent with a resource-based approach to early intervention (Trivette, Dunst, & Deal, 1997), which recognizes that communities are sources of support for meeting the needs of children and families. Such information is critical to understanding inclusion in its broadest sense.

As service providers and families have recognized the importance of participation in communities for young children with disabilities, efforts to build community resources (Umsted, Boyd, & Dunst, 1995) and to deliver early intervention in community settings have begun to emerge

(Bruder, 1993; McLean & Hanline, 1990; Yellen-Shiring & Voss, 1996). However, there are few studies of inclusion in contexts outside of classroom and day care settings and little information about factors that influence the participation of children with disabilities in community settings (Beckman et al., 1998; Ehrmann, Aeschleman, & Svanum, 1995). Seeking to meet this need, several studies we conducted as part of the ECRII addressed the issue of children's participation in community settings.

WHAT FACTORS INFLUENCE PARTICIPATION IN COMMUNITY PROGRAMS?

In the ECRII studies, it became clear that many families made efforts to include their children in a wide variety of activities within the community. In addition to day care settings, parents described efforts to include their children in after-school programs, religious/spiritual groups, martial arts, scouting, park and recreation programs, library programs, camps, gymnastics, organized sports activities, dance, birthday parties, music lessons, neighborhood activities, and more. Parents described some of these efforts as successful, whereas they viewed others as frustrating and some as extremely difficult. When the program or activity was frustrating or difficult, parents frequently removed their children from it entirely, rather than continue to expose them to an experience that the parents perceived as hurtful. We were interested in what factors made the difference in the type of experience that parents described. The story of Gail's relationship with Angie and the friendship that developed between their daughters illustrates many of the important processes that can facilitate successful community experiences for young children with disabilities.

Underlying Philosophy of Community Programs

The underlying philosophy of the community program in which children participated often made a critical difference in the kind of experience children with disabilities had. The program philosophy typically was reflected in the underlying assumptions programs made about children's participation. If a program began with the assumption that all children belonged and that it was the program's responsibility to adapt to the needs of the children, it often approached activities in a very different way than if it made the assumption that children needed to fit into the program to order to participate. The importance of this fundamental philosophical difference was illustrated in the story that one Boy Scout leader told about the participation of Ned, a child with cerebral palsy who used a wheelchair. When his Boy Scout troop decided to go camping, the troop leader looked for campgrounds that had a campsite that was accessible to wheelchairs as well as an accessible bathroom. If she did not find one, the entire troop did not go camping. The fundamental assumption was that Ned was as much a part of this troop as any other child—he belonged—and the troop would not consider going camping without him. This philosophy contrasts sharply with one in which the child with a disability can participate only if he or she can manage to fit in or if the family can find ways to overcome obstacles to the child's participation.

Another key component of the program philosophy was the extent to which children were expected to demonstrate specific skills, particularly if they had to acquire these skills within a specific amount of time, or if children were grouped according to age. For example, several families reported positive experiences with martial arts programs in which all children, regardless of age, participated together, based on what they were learning at a particular time. In such programs, groups were often heterogeneous with respect to age and moved through the program at their own pace. In contrast, many organized sports activities were somewhat more problematic, at least partly because of the skills that children were expected to demonstrate. One mother was frustrated because when she tried to sign her son up for adapted baseball, she was told that he was not "disabled enough." When he was put on a team with typically developing children, the experience was painful for him and his parents because other parents were not supportive and the coach ignored him.

One Key Individual

In the vignette described at the beginning of this chapter, it was one key person, Angie, who made a difference in the kind of experience that Gail and Sarah had when they tried to attend church. As in many of the studies conducted through the ECRII, it was often the commitment of one key individual that made a difference in whether a child was able to participate in a particular community event, activity, or program. This individual might be a teacher or service provider, another parent, or a volunteer or staff member from a community program. The common characteristic of these individuals was that they were committed to the child's participation and often went out of their way to encourage it. They helped by bringing a positive attitude to the child's participation and by facilitating the child's participation in many different ways. Some provided parents with critical information at key moments—information about their rights and about options within the community. In some cases, these individuals became advocates for the child. In others, they helped families deal with issues of accessibility. For example, one mother who had two children in wheelchairs described the way in which a member of her church called her in advance of a church function to ask if the family needed assistance to attend. They worked together to figure out how tables at the church could be adapted to accommodate her children's wheelchairs. Another mother was not planning to have her child with disabilities participate in an outing with members of the church, even though her other children were planning to participate. When a staff member at the church asked why her son wasn't going, the mother said that he couldn't go because he couldn't walk. The staff member then offered to carry the child so that he could participate.

Attitude of Community Providers

One way in which particular individuals became key to facilitating children's participation in the community was their attitude. As described in our previous discussion of program philosophy, the most helpful attitudes frequently reflected an assumption that the child with the disability belonged simply because he or she was part of the community.

Another important attitude that appeared to promote children's participation in community settings was a willingness on the part of staff members to experiment and explore solutions. Such staff members were typically open to suggestions from parents and worked actively with parents to explore new possibilities. As indicated in the examples about accommodations, it was also helpful when volunteers and staff members in community programs were sensitive to the possibility that families might need special accommodations and worked with family members to find solutions.

However, when staff members and volunteers approached the participation of a child with a disability with concern and fear, parents often found participation to be a struggle. This frequently was reflected in responses to a particular label (e.g., autism). In some cases, community providers simply assumed that a child would be unable to participate because of the label that had been assigned. This frustrated parents who wanted providers to get to know the individual skills, interests, and personality characteristics of their child. At other times, staff members feared responsibility for particular medical or caregiving needs. While parents understood many of these fears, they frequently emphasized the importance of learning about the child rather than simply responding to the label.

Parents' Strategies

Many of the families in our studies made special efforts to ensure that their children had the opportunity to participate in community settings and to develop friendships with other children. Although their strategies varied based on the resources that they had at their disposal, as well as on the individual needs of their children, they frequently shared a common belief that they needed to work actively to ensure that their children had the opportunity to participate.

Families promoted their children's participation in community settings in multiple ways, many of which were quite inventive. They frequently learned about potential activities and programs by talking to other parents—several parents particularly emphasized the value of word-of-mouth information about activities, events, and programs that might be of interest to their children.

Many parents thought carefully about how to approach community leaders in a way that would ensure that their child would be allowed to participate. One area of particular concern was if and how they would describe the child's disability. Several parents reported that they often did not tell community providers about their child's disability until they had already enrolled the child in the program—previous experience had taught them that community providers might respond negatively to the child's label before getting to know the child. They wanted community providers to get to know their child—"fall in love" with the child—and then they could work together to plan accommodations. Other parents took the opposite approach, wanting to make sure that the community providers knew what the child's needs would be. One mother said, "I always make it [the disability] sound worse." She reasoned that then, when people meet her child, they are pleasantly surprised.

Some strategies that parents used were designed to convince community providers to allow their child to participate or to convince school officials that a community placement was an acceptable alternative to a more segregated placement. Sometimes, they had to overcome policies that prevented their child's participation, in some cases by actively advocating and reminding providers about legal requirements. One child with Down syndrome had been successfully included in an early intervention day care program for infants. However, when she began receiving services as a preschooler, the school system wanted her to receive them in a segregated program. This mother successfully advocated for her child to continue to be served at the day care center, by challenging the school decision through due process provisions.

Other strategies were designed to make children's participation in the program, event, or activity successful once they were accepted. For example, several parents reported that they volunteered in the program in which their child was participating. By volunteering, they could observe how their child was doing, work with staff and volunteers, and intervene if their child was experiencing difficulties. One parent volunteered so that she would be available in the event that staff members or other children had questions.

Noting that many staff members in community programs lack training and experience with children who have special needs, several parents worked actively with program staff to help them understand the child's needs. Examples of such efforts included making presentations about their child's special needs to staff, demonstrating ways to feed and handle the child, and showing staff how to manage particular behaviors. Others held question-and-answer sessions with other children in the program. They felt that this would help prevent teasing and other negative exchanges with peers and would help promote understanding and acceptance.

Still other strategies were focused on encouraging friendships within the neighborhoods, communities, and programs in which children participated. For example, one father bought tickets to sporting events and invited other children who were the same age as his son with autism. He felt that this motivated the other children to be with his son and provided social opportunities for his son. Another father promoted social contact for his daughter with Down syndrome by building on other children's interest in playing with her younger sister. In the vignette described at the opening of this chapter, Gail made a point of inviting Angie's daughter, Kelsie, over for a play date. This was the beginning of a friendship between the girls that eventually spilled over into other areas of their lives.

Some parents emphasized the importance of getting to know other parents in the program, particularly parents of children that they knew their child liked. They did this as a way of encouraging friendships between the children. Additionally, other parents were often a source of information about the program. Parents also arranged play dates, shopping excursions, and other joint outings to provide their children with opportunities for social contact with other children.

Adaptations

Parents repeatedly identified the availability of environmental adaptations as a critical factor influencing their children's ability to participate in community programs. When adaptations were available, they facilitated children's participation; when they were not, their absence frequently

made it frustrating, if not completely impossible, for children to participate.

Although some children needed extensive adaptations, most of the
adaptations that were needed were relatively small. For example, one
little boy who was diagnosed with pervasive developmental disorder
participated in a martial arts program. The only adaptation that he needed
in order to participate was to be placed in the front row so that he could
see the instructor and see himself and the other children in the mirror.
The family of another child was able to participate in a church function
because volunteers at the church helped the family raise a table enough
to accommodate their son's wheelchair.

Although the availability of adaptations often made the difference
in whether a child was physically able to participate in a particular event
or activity, the willingness of community leaders to work with families
to adapt materials and activities was important in another way as well.
Often, the willingness to learn about and make adaptations represented
a level of openness and acceptance that made parents feel as if their child
was welcome.

Communication

Another factor that appeared to influence children's participation in community programs was the ability of staff members and volunteers to
communicate effectively with families. The need to communicate centered
on many different aspects of children's participation, including the expectations that parents and community providers had of the child and of
one another, how to appropriately adapt activities for the child, and how
to manage the child's behavior. Many programs relied on volunteers or
relatively low-paid staff members who had little training or experience
with disabilities. This sometimes made communication between parents
and community providers difficult, and parents frequently had to take
the initiative in communicating.

Interconnections

When children and families knew each other in multiple contexts, this
familiarity often facilitated children's participation across contexts. In one
example taken from the ecological systems study, such interconnections
helped to mediate a potentially difficult situation when a little boy with
autism, Adam, bit Ellie, a little girl without disabilities in his preschool
class. These two children not only attended the same preschool program,
but went to the same neighborhood pool in the summer and lived in

the same neighborhood, and their parents were friends. Adam's parents immediately called Ellie's to apologize, and received a warm and understanding response. When Ellie was asked why he bit her, she explained that she thought it was because "he likes me so much." In this instance, knowing one another in multiple contexts provided a broader frame of reference for children and families when something went wrong (Beckman et al., 1998).

The importance of interconnections also was described by focus-group participants in the community study. Ned, a boy with cerebral palsy, became friends with Mark, who did not have disabilities, through their common participation in church and in Boy Scouts. Mark's mother was the troop leader and learned about the adaptations Ned needed in order to participate in various activities. As a result, she was sensitive to the family's need for adaptations in other activities and often called Ned's mother in advance of these activities to make sure that Ned and his family could participate.

IMPLICATIONS FOR PRACTICE

The factors described earlier have many implications for service providers and community leaders who work with young children who have disabilities. One important implication is that volunteers and staff members in community programs need to examine the philosophy that is at the heart of the programs in which they work. There is a need for them to question assumptions that work to exclude children with disabilities.

Another implication is that providers need to be aware of the important difference that they, as individuals, can make in the lives of young children with disabilities and their families. Even if a program discourages participation, an individual who works in the program often can make the difference in the type of experiences parents and families have. Individuals can make this difference by being sensitive to the needs of the child and the family, by going out of their way to learn about those needs, by providing information, by using good communication skills, and when necessary, by advocating on behalf of a particular child and family. One particularly important way in which individuals can make a difference is by setting a tone of acceptance—one that can be conveyed through the language they use about a particular child and through the assumptions they make about children.

The importance of communication is reported frequently in studies of families of children with disabilities and certainly is not unique to community participation. However, in community programs, many special issues may affect communication. Because of limited financial re-sources, many community programs (e.g., day care, recreation programs) struggle with relatively high turnover rates and the need to continually train new staff or volunteers who may have limited experience with disabilities and little awareness of the issues facing families. In some instances, this may lead to fear, frustration, and insensitivity. Program leaders can help by recognizing the importance of effective communica-tion with families and by providing staff and volunteers with opportuni-ties for training.

Finally, as individuals, service providers can help families develop their own strategies for working within the context of community pro-grams. This can be done by providing families with information and resources that they can take to the community programs in which they participate. Such information may include knowledge about their rights under the Americans with Disabilities Act and knowledge of resources that might help volunteers and staff members in community programs better meet the needs of children. Service providers also can help family members identify critical questions to ask community leaders when they are considering a new program for their child.

CONCLUSION

As community programs increasingly include young children with disa-bilities, families as well as staff members and volunteers face new chal-lenges. The studies conducted as part of the ECRII suggest that while some of the challenges are similar to those that have been experienced in educational settings (e.g., issues related to individual attitudes and making appropriate adaptations), others are unique to community-based programs (e.g., how to provide appropriate training for volunteers). Deal-ing appropriately with these challenges is essential to ensuring that chil-dren with disabilities become truly included in their communities.

REFERENCES

Amado, A. (1993). Steps for supporting community connections. In A. Amado (Ed.), *Friendships and community connections between people with and without disabilities* (pp. 299–326). Baltimore, MD: Brookes.

Beckman, P. J., Barnwell, D., Horn, E., Hanson, M. J., Gutierrez, S., & Lieber, J. (1998). Communities, families, and inclusion. *Early Childhood Research Quar-terly, 13,* 125–150.

Bruder, M. B. (1993). The provision of early intervention and early childhood special education within community early childhood programs: Characteristics of effective service delivery. *Topics in Early Childhood Special Education, 12*, 119–137.

Day, M. (2000). *Supporting inclusion of young children with disabilities in community settings.* Unpublished doctoral dissertation, University of Maryland, College Park.

Ehrmann, L., Aeschleman, S., & Svanum, S. (1995). Parental reports of community activity patterns: A comparison between young children with disabilities and their nondisabled peers. *Research on Developmental Disabilities, 16*, 331–343.

McLean, M., & Hanline, M. F. (1990). Providing early intervention services in integrated environments: Challenges and opportunities for the future. *Topics in Early Childhood Special Education, 10*, 62–77.

Moon, M. S. (1994). The case for inclusive school and community recreation. In M. S. Moon (Ed.), *Making school and community recreation fun for everyone* (pp. 1–16). Baltimore, MD: Brookes.

Trivette, C. M., Dunst, C. J., & Deal, A. G. (1997). Resource-based approach to early intervention. In S. K. Thurman, J. R. Cornwell, & S. R. Gottwald (Eds.), *Contexts of early intervention: Systems and settings* (pp. 73–92). Baltimore, MD: Brookes.

Turnbull, A .P., Turnbull, H. R., & Blue-Banning, M. (1994). Enhancing inclusion of infants and toddlers with disabilities and their families: A theoretical and programmatic analysis. *Infants and Young Children, 7*(2), 1–14.

Umsted, S., Boyd, S., & Dunst, C. (1995, July). Building community resources: Enabling inclusion in community programs and activities. *Exceptional Parent,* pp. 36–37.

Wellman, B., & Leighton, B. (1979, July). Networks, neighborhoods, and communities: Approaches to the study of the community question. *Urban Affairs Quarterly,* pp. 36–37.

Yellen-Shiring, G., & Voss, S. (1996, December). *Enhancing community-based options in a family-centered early intervention program.* Presented at the Annual Conference of the Council from Exceptional Children Division for Early Childhood, Phoenix, AZ.

CHAPTER 9

Social Policy and Preschool Inclusion

Samuel L. Odom, Ruth A. Wolery,
Joan Lieber, & Eva Horn

WHEN KEVIN, THE CHILD WITH DOWN SYNDROME described in Chapter 5, entered his classroom at the Wesley Center preschool class (part of the VIP program) on his first day, a lot of work had gone into paving the way for his steps through the front door. Changes in services provided through the VIP program began a few years earlier when a local task force proposed that young children with disabilities should be included in programs for typically developing children rather than being enrolled only in segregated preschool classes. At about the same time, the VIP school system recruited a new superintendent of schools who appointed a supervisor of special education. This supervisor was much more open to providing inclusive services than was her predecessor. She appointed an early childhood coordinator and charged him with the responsibility of creating a pilot program that not only placed children with disabilities in child care programs throughout the community, but also provided their tuition, transportation, and special education support from an itinerant teacher. Not surprisingly, this program was well received in the community, and the VIP supervisor and staff were overwhelmed with parents requesting this service for their children. In fact, they received twice as many requests as they had placement opportunities! When we watched Kevin hang his coat in his cubby and turn around to see what his day in this new place has in store, we needed to recognize how the thoughts, actions, and decisions of many individuals contributed to that moment.

These thoughts, actions, and decisions, and how they are represented in written documents, are the essence of social policy. The mechanics of social policy occur outside of classroom settings, but they influence greatly the way classes and services for young children are planned and provided. In our research to identify barriers to and facilitators of preschool inclusion, we studied how social policy both affects inclusion and is affected by inclusion. We learned a lot about policy issues in different organizational contexts (community-based, Head Start, and public school programs), about key influences for beginning inclusive programs in a school system, and about factors that lead to the ongoing provision of preschool services or the termination of those services. Also, to answer questions posed by some administrators, we studied the costs of preschool inclusion. We investigated different program features that contribute to overall costs and ways administrators fund inclusive programs. In this chapter we discuss the areas of our research that relate to the influences of policy.

ORGANIZATIONAL CONTEXTS

As the examples we have used throughout this book indicate, inclusion occurs for young children with disabilities in community-based child care programs, Head Start programs, and public school early childhood programs. Each of these programs is located in a different type of organization, and the social policy and administrative issues for each are unique. The issues, as well as innovative solutions, are described in detail in Wolery and Odom (2000) and are summarized briefly here.

Community-based Programs

In community-based programs, school systems provide services to children with disabilities in privately owned or nonprofit child care settings operating outside of the public schools. The advantage of these programs, aside from access to classes in which there are typically developing children, is that they may be located in the child's and family's own community, and they may reflect, to some extent, great opportunity for family choice. To create community-based programs, however, school systems must adopt policies to allow services to be provided outside of the public school building; most state and local programs have now adopted such policies, although it was not true when we began our research. Furthermore, decisions about who pays tuition to the community-based program must be made. Sometimes, state policies prohibit local school systems from paying tuition to private child care centers; in these programs parents absorb the tuition costs. Sometimes a state policy will allow programs to pay tuition for an "educationally relevant" portion (e.g., 2½ to 3 hours) of the day in which the child is in the child care center. We found this option working in two of our programs, VIP and Lincoln County. A last issue is transportation. In our study we found a few programs that transported children to and from their home to the child care center, and in other programs parents provided the transportation. In the latter case, the parents absorbed the cost of transportation.

Head Start Programs

For Head Start, national policy requires programs to enroll children with disabilities. In some cases, Head Start agencies collaborated actively with the school systems. Such collaboration was fostered by open communication, sharing of resources, and joint planning and input from respective staffs and administrators. For example, one public school administrator told us:

> Our preschool and Head Start are very much a part of our school family. They are included on our teams even though they technically are just housed in our building. We try hard to make them feel a part . . . and in terms of Kenny [a child with disabilities] we all see it as our role to make him fit in—to just be a part of the group. (Wolery & Odom, 2000, p. 34)

In other programs, children with disabilities were enrolled in Head Start but had very little contact with individuals from the public school systems. The challenge for these programs was to establish relationships that would allow the Head Start program to draw on the expertise of special education teachers and related service providers who worked for the public school.

Other issues also exist for some Head Start programs that include children with disabilities. The schedules and regulations for Head Start programs and public schools are different, which requires some flexibility on the part of both agencies. Head Start has an income criterion that families must meet. For children with disabilities whose family incomes are above the criterion, Head Start programs have a limited number of income waivers that allow those families to participate. As described previously, Head Start and public school organizations sometimes have different teaching philosophies. Administrative support for collaborative planning has helped some programs bridge such philosophical differences.

Public School Programs

Some public schools do provide classes for typically developing preschool-aged children, and such classes have been used as inclusive class placements for children with disabilities. One policy issue we saw in several programs resulted in administrative resistance within the system. This occurred when the early childhood programs were administratively housed in a department or branch of the school system other than special education. A solution, which occurred in the Lincoln County program, was to move all programs for young children into the same administrative department and to create a clear mission statement that all young children should be included in the early childhood programs. Public schools also have created their own tuition-based child care or preschool classes to serve children in the community. To facilitate inclusion, parents of children with disabilities can enroll their children into these classes at no charge. We found that when these programs were established, administrative arrangements had to be made to receive and use funds from the public. Last, in some public school programs, space is a major barrier. We found that while program administrators were open to establishing preschool classes that could become inclusive sites within the school systems, if they did not have the space in their buildings, their interest was reduced.

STARTING AND IMPLEMENTING INCLUSIVE PROGRAMS

When we began our research, inclusion at the preschool level was just beginning to be provided as an option for children with disabilities in many of the programs with which we worked, although there were some notable exceptions (e.g., Lincoln County, Vista Valley). Fullan (2001) noted that when a new type of service is started, it often is called an "innovation." So as one of our early tasks, we began searching for the influences that allowed this innovation to start (or continue to work well) in our group of 16 inclusive preschool programs.

Across our programs, we found there were several factors that influenced whether preschool inclusion began, and we also found that these same factors potentially served as barriers when they were absent (Lieber et al., 2000). The first and strongest facilitator of inclusion was having *key personnel* in positions to influence policy. Sometimes this occurred at the school system level. For example, in Lincoln County, the superintendent of schools believed that

> A preschool experience should be available to every child or family that wishes it; that children shouldn't be transported beyond programs for which they don't qualify to others that they do; and that they should be attending their neighborhood schools. (Lieber et al., 2000, p. 91)

This superintendent's belief, like that of the superintendent in the VIP program, shaped the way services were provided to children. In other programs, the key person was a leader at the building level. In the Beacon Street program, the driving force was the principal. Teachers told us: "The principal approached us . . . about co-teaching and doing an inclusion program. She gave us the opportunity to design it and do it any way we wanted to" (Lieber et al., 2000, p. 89). In still other programs, this innovation was supported at the classroom level. At Valley View, for example, a teacher began including young children with disabilities in an early childhood program that had been operating in a high school for 10 years.

Another key influence on whether preschool inclusion occurred, was a *shared vision* among special education and early childhood education staff or agencies. In two of our programs, a preschool inclusion task force composed of individuals from the school system and local Head Start agency jointly developed their program philosophy and definition of inclusion. We also found that a common perspective among classroom staff on the purposes of the inclusive program for both children with and children without disabilities was very important (more information on this point is provided in Chapter 6). When this shared vision was not present, as in Northumberland's Winter County co-teaching classroom that involved both Head Start and special education teachers, we found that staff were under considerable stress.

A third key influence on starting inclusive preschool programs was *state and national policy.* In Lincoln County, for example, there was significant influence from the Kentucky Education Reform Act (KERA). The director of the early childhood program told us: "The goal of the State KERA preschool program was to make sure that children are served . . . in typical classrooms. So we didn't even consider another model. It was never an issue" (Lieber et al., 2000, p. 94). In the Northumberland program, the Head Start director informed us that the national Head Start policy of including children with disabilities directly influenced the program's plans for collaborating with the public schools to create inclusive preschool programs.

Program directors sometimes used *training/external support* to promote preschool inclusion. For example, when administrators from the VIP program first considered providing an inclusive option for children, local administrators and teachers visited the Lincoln County program, which had been established several years earlier. The old adage "seeing is believing" had an important influence on VIP's plans for inclusion. Taking advantage of both training and external support, the preschool coordinator at Cornwallis increased the number of inclusive classrooms in her program by applying for and receiving funds from the state government for a week-long summer training workshop. This led to new classrooms being started the following year.

We also found that the *organizational structure* of a program or agency was a key influence over the occurrence of preschool inclusion. Sometimes, the organizational structures were formally linked through interagency agreements. In the Vista Valley program, for example, the Head Start director told us:

> We started with a simple interagency agreement that was embellished and grew as we learned more about what each program had to offer . . . leading up to the point of needing to get beyond our level to the level of the Board of Education and the superintendent. Making sure that they were aware of the kinds of programs we were trying to develop . . . and the kind of fiscal support that we needed from their level [was important]. (Lieber et al., 2000, p. 95)

Last, *community influences* played a role in establishing inclusive preschool programs. We found that parents were particularly influential in facilitating the provision of inclusive services. A Rolling Hills mother, for example, insisted that her child with a physical disability be allowed to attend the Head Start program in her community rather than a segregated special education program provided by the public school. This parent's advocacy led to an educational assistant being assigned to the Head Start program to work with several children with disabilities who attended that classroom. Community influence also was found in the VIP program, where a range of members from the community constituted the preschool task force that played such an important role in establishing inclusion in that system.

In summary, innovation in public schools is notoriously slow in coming. But for individuals committed to change, it is important to know that there may be ways to "speed up the process." Ensuring that key individuals in the system can serve as advocates, establishing a shared vision among teachers and parents, building on existing national and state policy, planning an organizational structure to unlie the innovation, and marshalling community influences are all strategies that may be used.

MAINTENANCE OF PRESCHOOL INCLUSION

The information on key influences came from our interviews and observations during the first 2 years of our research. This information told us how inclusive preschool programs got started or continued over a short period. We also were interested in how programs changed over a longer period. Did they become more or less inclusive? What factors influenced the changes? To answer these questions about the maintenance of preschool inclusion, we followed our 16 programs for another 3 years. We visited programs, observed, and interviewed administrators during the third year of our research and again in the fifth year, and we found that changes did occur and specific factors appeared to influence those changes (Horn et al., 2000).

When all the information collected on programs across the 5 years was reviewed, we found that two classrooms in the Northumberland program had taken very different directions, and we decided to separate the information for our analysis (which created 17 programs for our analysis rather than the 16 originally mentioned). We also found that among the programs, different patterns of change had occurred over the 5-year period. Four of the programs experienced *growth*, meaning that the number of children in inclusive programs and the number of inclusive options were larger at the end of the 5 years. For example, the VIP program had evolved from a small community-based program to a program providing nearly all preschool services to children with disabilities in a variety of inclusive settings.

Another pattern we found was *stability*, which we defined as programs that (1) began with a strong commitment to preschool inclusion, (2) responded to changes in community needs, and (3) expressed a clear commitment to continuing inclusive options into the future. Six of our programs had stability at the end of 5 years. When we began our research, the large urban/suburban system, Lincoln County, for example, already had inclusive placements for most of the preschool children served. At the end of the 5 years, they continued to provide such services; however, the nature of the services had shifted more toward a public school model than a community-based model.

For seven of the programs we observed, however, the trend was in the opposite direction. At the end of 5 years, six of our programs showed *minimal* change and commitment to inclusion at the preschool level. Information we collected from these programs showed that from the beginning, there was limited commitment from teachers, other staff, and administrators, along with little push for inclusion from within the system. With two systems operating independently of each other, as in Santa Luna, there was very little interaction between Head Start teachers and staff and the public school teacher and administrators.

In our 5-year study, we also had one inclusive classroom that closed after the first year of our research. We called this *regression*, meaning (1) loss of commitment by the school system for preschool inclusion, (2) children being placed in less inclusive settings, and (3) loss of interagency collaboration. The Winter County classroom in the Northumberland program did not reopen after the first year. The public school and Head Start administrators decided to discontinue the team teaching option due to administrative and staff issues, resulting in the public school returning to a model of delivering preschool services for children with disabilities in segregated settings.

To understand what led to changes across the years, we grouped the programs that had gone in a positive direction (growth and stability programs) and the programs that had gone in a negative direction (minimal and regression programs). Our researchers then described and analyzed events that occurred in these two program groups over the period of time we were involved with them. From this analysis, we identified themes that influenced the direction programs took.

Themes Related to Stability and Growth

Four common themes emerged from our study of programs that grew or remained strong and stable over the 5 years of our study.

1. The programs began with a strong commitment to inclusion, that is, they had a "critical mass" of individuals who supported inclusion.
2. The programs had a balance between support and pressure for inclusion from different parts of the system.
3. The programs adapted their beliefs and actions in response to changes in the programs or community.
4. The programs had a broad-based ownership of inclusion.

The Vista Valley program portrays a program that reflected growth. In this program children with disabilities were included in classes in a Head Start center, and an itinerant special education teacher was assigned to the center 3–4 hours each day. There was a strong and assertive interest from both Head Start and public school administrators (i.e., a critical mass of support). Furthermore, a full-inclusion task force, which included individuals from different agencies, had been involved in the planning stages and remained involved across the years (i.e., support and pressure for inclusion). Over the 5 years of our study, the public school system expanded its inclusive options into community-based programs, but maintained its collaborative relationship with Head Start (i.e., adapted actions across time). Midway through our research, the administrators from the public schools and Head Start renewed their commitment to "make it work" (i.e., broad-based ownership). By the end of our observations, additional inclusive Head Start sites had opened that used the same collaborative approach with the public schools. In fact, by the final year of our study, public school special education teachers were working as resource specialists in almost every Head Start program in the county. For us, Vista Valley was a success story!

Themes Related to Minimal Change and Regression

Programs that did not become success stories also shared several characteristics. Each of these programs began with a *limited commitment to inclusion* from the school systems. Costa Mesa, for example, was committed to providing an integrative-activities approach to inclusion. In this approach, children with disabilities and typically developing children were located in separate classrooms. A flexible wall separated the two classrooms. For a portion of the day, the teachers opened up the divider for the two groups to combine for integrated/inclusive activities, and the children returned to their respective classes after the inclusion period. The groups also participated jointly in other activities during the day, such as lunch, outdoor play, and weekly field trips. We interpreted this form of inclusion as being a more limited commitment to inclusion than occurred in other programs. Across the 5 years of our study, the program never moved to an approach in which children with and without disabilities shared the same classroom for the entire class session.

A second theme of programs that took a negative direction was *limited pressure for inclusion*. In the Rolling Hills program, there was interest on the part of Head Start administrators to enroll children with disabilities, but they were unable to exert pressure on the public school system, where administrators were not interested in moving "their children" into Head Start or any other inclusive option.

A third theme of minimal change and regression programs was *limited support for inclusion*. We found evidence of this in the Costa Mesa program, where Head Start teachers told us they knew very little about children with disabilities, and the public schools and Head Start were not providing them with needed training and support.

The classroom that did not reopen after the first year of our study was part of the large Northumberland program, in which a Head Start program collaborated with two different school systems to provide a team teaching model of preschool inclusion. Although the Winter County classroom began with some preplanning between Head Start and the two public school agencies during the year before the program began, the administrators assigned teachers to this classroom. The teachers later told us they had not known what they were getting into. In fact, around midyear, the Head Start teacher attended a workshop on inclusion, and after the workshop she told us she would not have agreed to participate in the inclusion program if she had known what was involved. Furthermore, although the teachers were identified before the co-teaching arrangement began, they were not provided an opportunity to jointly plan for the coming year. And, to complicate the situation even more, the public school program began 3 weeks before the Head Start program, so the Head Start teacher and children returned to find their classroom rearranged and inhabited by a teacher and children they did not know.

Despite the fact that this inclusion effort got off to a bad start, attempts were made to have joint planning sessions and to agree upon responsibilities. Differing philosophies, however, created a major barrier that was hard to overcome. The Head Start teacher and teaching assistant were tied to an early childhood education curriculum that their agency insisted they follow. The special education teacher and her teaching assistant felt that children with disabilities needed some time each day in individualized and small-group instruction. This led to conflict between teachers and their administrators. Over the year, conflicts between Head Start and special education increased, and by midyear when we left, there was considerable tension, which could not be diffused by actions of the administrators.

Although personal and professional differences contributed strongly to the regression that occurred in Winter County, the themes previously noted also were apparent. First, there was limited commitment to inclusion; this classroom was the only inclusive preschool program in the Winter County system. Second, there was limited pressure for inclusion; few key public school administrators were actively supportive of the program (although there were no major opponents to the class). Finally, there was limited support in terms of training, planning time, flexible regulations, and scheduling.

COSTS OF PRESCHOOL INCLUSION

Social policy, as Jim Gallagher (1994) describes it, is the process of "distributing finite resources to meet infinite needs" (p. 337). Policy makers, like local supervisors of special education, coordinators of state and national agencies, directors of early childhood programs, and directors of Head Start agencies, make decisions about the types of services that their programs will offer to children and families. In making these decisions, they have to balance the needs of children and families with the costs of the programs.

When we talked with administrators, one of the questions that sometimes came up was about costs (Janko & Porter, 1997). That is, administrators were concerned that inclusive preschool programs might cost more than traditional segregated special education programs. In some systems, the perception that inclusive preschool programs were more expensive than traditional special education programs was a barrier. Yet, when we looked at policy analyses and published research on preschool inclusion, we could find no information about how much such programs cost.

To learn more about the costs of preschool inclusion, we contacted four programs (one from each site) that were in our original ecological systems study and one additional program from North Carolina. Because we knew that preschool inclusion takes different forms (Odom et al., 1999), we selected programs that were located in different organizational contexts and used different individualized-service models. We asked administrators and teachers to help us choose at least seven children with

Table 9.1. Mean Service Delivery Hours, Total Instructional Costs, and Costs to School Districts for Five Programs in Inclusive and Traditional Segregated Settings

Program	Mean Weekly Service Delivery Hours[a]	Total Instructional Costs ($)		Costs to School District ($)	
		Annual	Per Service Hour	Annual	Per Service Hour
Program A					
Head Start (IT)	22.5	$5,108^b$	6.60^c	$2,151^c$	2.78^c
Comm.-based (IT)	17.0	$2,647^c$	4.52^c	$1,319^c$	2.25^c
Traditional	15.7	3,817	7.08	3,079	5.70
Program B					
Public school (TT)	12.5	$3,763^c$	8.63^b	$3,763^c$	8.63^b
Traditional	15.0	3,886	7.19	3,886	7.19
Program C					
Comm.-based (IT)	23.1	$4,364^c$	5.24^b	$1,325^c$	1.59^c
Traditional	31.2	5,650	5.03	4,963	4.42
Program D					
Comm.-based (IT)	21.3	$4,864^c$	8.03^c	$4,863^b$	6.34^c
Comm.-based (TT)	16.2	$6,999^b$	12.00^b	$6,886^b$	11.80^b
Public school (IA)	14.9	$2,609^c$	3.60^c	$2,609^c$	3.24^c
Traditional	15.1	4,521	8.31	4,521	8.17
Program E					
Public school (TB)	12.0	$1,203^c$	2.75^c	941^c	2.17
Head Start (IT)	11.6	$1,687^c$	4.03^c	$1,687^b$	4.03^b
Traditional	11.3	1,936	4.75	1,576	3.87

Notes. IT = itinerant teacher; TT = team teaching; IA = integrative activities; TB = tuition based. Adapted with permission from "The Costs of Preschool Inclusion," by S. L. Odom et al., 2001, *Topics in Early Childhood Special Education, 21*, pp. 46-55. Copyright 2001 by PRO-ED, Inc.

[a] Program A was in operation 34.4 weeks per year; programs B, C, D, and E were in operation 36 weeks per year.

[b] Cost less than traditional program.

[c] Cost more than traditional program.

disabilities who were enrolled in the preschool classes and at least seven children who were the same age and had similar disabilities but were enrolled in traditional segregated classes.

To gather the cost information, we worked with the Center for Special Education Finance (at the American Institutes for Research in Palo Alto, CA) to create three interview questionnaires that provided information about the costs of services related to instruction (e.g., teacher salaries, equipment, materials). From these interviews with teachers, related service providers, and administrators, we were able to calculate the average costs per child as well as the cost per service hour. A detailed description of this methodology can be found in Odom and colleagues (2001).

The main findings of our study appear in Table 9.1. Different programs provided different types of inclusive services for children, with some providing a community-based/itinerant teacher model, some a Head Start/itinerant teacher model, others a community-based team teaching model, and still others an integrative-activities model in public schools. Three of the programs provided more than one form of inclusion.

We computed both total costs for the inclusive and traditional models, and also costs only to the school district (i.e., in some cases the public schools were only one of several agencies contributing funds for the inclusive program). When we compared the costs of inclusion with traditional programs, we found that inclusive programs were less expensive in six of the nine comparisons. The community-based/itinerant teacher models tended to be the least expensive of the inclusive models, if the school system did not pay the tuition for the child to attend the community-based program, but they also provided the least amount of time and contact with a special education teacher. In a reanalysis of these cost data (Odom, Parrish, & Hikido, in press), we grouped the costs by inclusive and traditional programs, and found the total cost per service hour was about 8% less for inclusive programs than for traditional special education programs ($5.77 vs. $6.28).

Although we felt that this study provided useful information about costs for a small number of programs, we were disappointed that there were some things we could not control or about which we could not obtain information. The school system staff could not give us information about the costs for children's transportation and for building costs (e.g., rent or depreciation, utilities, maintenance). So while the total costs and cost to the school district were useful for comparing inclusive with traditional programs, they did not convey the entire costs that school districts pay for either type of program. Also, we tried to find comparable groups of children in inclusive and traditional special education programs, but it is possible that the children in the traditional special education classes had more severe disabilities.

To help administrators compute the costs for their local districts, we described the cost features in different inclusive and traditional programs. These appear in Table 9.2. Teachers' salaries are always a major cost for programs, but in different models of inclusion different teachers or staff are involved. For example, in the community-based itinerant model, an itinerant teacher is involved, but the school district does not pay for the early childhood education teacher's salary (unless the district pays the child care tuition). When this salary is distributed over a large number of children located in community settings, the per-child salary cost decreases. In contrast, in a team teaching model, the school district usually pays for the special education teacher and an assistant, but the teacher may be responsible for fewer children with disabilities, which may increase the salary costs per child. In some models, transportation for the teacher is a cost, while in other models, transportation for children is more prominent. When considering whether to begin an inclusive preschool program, an administrator might project the costs of the features identified in Table 9.2 to estimate costs at the local school district.

FINANCING PRESCHOOL INCLUSION

Our research suggests that inclusive services for children with disabilities do not cost more than traditional segregated special education services, and in some cases they may be less expensive. However, a second issue about cost is how preschool administrators fund the programs. We found that administrators' flexibility and creativity in arranging finances were important for the success of preschool inclusion. Some solutions that administrators found for financing inclusive programs are briefly described in the next section, and more detail is provided in Wolery and Odom (2000).

IMPLICATIONS FOR PRACTICE

From the research on social policy, there are a number of practical recommendations for beginning, maintaining, and funding programs.

To Start an Inclusive Preschool Program

- Be sure to have the support of key administrators in the system
- Involve teachers and other classroom professionals early in planning the program
- Develop a shared vision of preschool inclusion for all involved

Table 9.2. Cost Features for Inclusive and Traditional Special Education Models

Program Costs to School System	Community Based—IT (Programs A, C, D)	Community Based—TT (Program D)	Head Start—IT (Programs A, E)	Public School—TT (Program B)	Public School—TB (Program E)	Public School—IA (Program D)	Traditional (All Programs)
Itinerant special education teacher	✓						
Early childhood classroom teacher			✓	✓		✓	
Special education classroom teacher		✓		✓	✓	✓	✓
Paraprofessional		✓		✓	✓	✓	✓
Related service personnel	✓	✓	✓	✓	✓	✓	✓
Child care tuition	✓[a]	✓					
Transportation for child	✓[a]	✓	✓	✓	✓	✓	✓
Transportation for teacher	✓		✓				
Equipment				✓	✓	✓	✓
Materials				✓	✓	✓	✓
Building costs				✓	✓	✓	✓
Administrative costs	✓	✓	✓	✓	✓	✓	✓

Notes. IT = itinerant teacher; TT = team teaching; TB = tuition based; IA = integrative activities. Reprinted with permission from "The Costs of Preschool Inclusion," by S. L. Odom et al., 2001, *Topics in Early Childhood Special Education, 21*, pp. 46–55. Copyright 2001 by PRO-ED, Inc.
[a] Not provided in all programs.

- Provide training and administrative support for program staff
- Build on community support (e.g., task force with parents, teachers, program providers)
- Establish a "structure" in the organization that supports inclusion (e.g., cooperative agreements)

To Maintain an Inclusive Preschool Program

- Have an ongoing "critical mass" to lead and support the program
- Be flexible and respond to change in the community (e.g., provide different inclusive options based on family/community needs)
- Build joint ownership of the program across agencies and community members
- Be aware of the different policy influences that operate in different organizational contexts

To Finance Preschool Inclusion

- Provide child care tuition for an educationally relevant portion of the day for placements of children with disabilities in community-based programs
- Include children with disabilities in state-funded "pre-K" programs for children from low-income families
- Access state funding for child care to pay tuition of children with disabilities placed in community-based programs
- Establish agreements between Head Start and public schools that allow children with disabilities to be carried on both their rolls and that guarantee placement for children with disabilities whose families meet the Head Start income criterion
- Arrange for the Head Start income waiver to be applied for children with disabilities whose family incomes are above the income criterion
- Assist families of children with disabilities to apply for "sliding scale" tuition that some community-based program have for families not meeting the low-income criterion
- Enroll children with disabilities in Title 1 preschool programs operating in public schools
- Create tuition-based preschool programs for typically developing children in the community and enroll children with disabilities at no cost to the parents
- Place children with disabilities in child care or preschool programs that operate in high schools

In conclusion, as Kevin picked up his backpack and walked with his teacher out to his bus, and when he returned on his second, third, and fourth days, the thoughts, decisions, and actions of adults outside of the class continued to provide the necessary support for his class placement. They worked out ways for his itinerant teacher to make visits to the program, to pay for his attendance, and to provide his transportation. Without these invisible supports, inclusion for Kevin would not have been possible.

REFERENCES

Fullan, M. G. (2001). *The new meaning of educational change* (3rd ed.). New York: Teachers College Press.

Gallagher, J. (1994). Policy designed for diversity: New initiatives for children with disabilities. In D. Bryant & M. Graham (Eds.), *Implementing early intervention* (pp. 336–350). New York: Guilford Press.

Horn, E., Lieber, J., Sandall, S., Hanson, M. J., Schwartz, I. S., & Odom, S. L. (2000). *Maintenance of preschool inclusion.* Manuscript in preparation.

Janko, S. J., & Porter, A. (1997). *Portraits of inclusion through the eyes of children, families, and educators.* Seattle, WA: Early Childhood Research Institute on Inclusion.

Lieber, J., Hanson, M. J., Beckman, P. J., Odom, S. L., Sandall, S. R., Schwartz, I. S., Horn, E., & Wolery, R. (2000). Key influences on the initiation and implementation of inclusive preschool programs. *Exceptional Children, 67,* 83–98.

Odom, S. L., Hanson, M. J., Lieber, J., Marquart, J., Sandall, S., Wolery, R., Horn, E., Schwartz, I., Beckman, P., Hikido, C., & Chambers, J. (2001). The costs of preschool inclusion. *Topics in Early Childhood Special Education, 21,* 46–55.

Odom, S. L., Horn, E. M., Marquart, J., Hanson, M. J., Wolfberg, P., Beckman, P. J., Lieber, J., Li, S., Schwartz, I., Janko, S., & Sandall, S. (1999). On the forms of inclusion: Organizational context and individualized service delivery models. *Journal of Early Intervention, 22,* 185–199.

Odom, S. L., Parrish, T., & Hikido, C. (in press). The costs of inclusive and traditional special education preschool services. *Journal of Special Education Leadership.*

Wolery, R. A., & Odom, S. L. (2000). *An administrator's guide to preschool inclusion.* Chapel Hill: University of North Carolina, Frank Porter Graham Child Development Center and the Early Childhood Research Institute on Inclusion.

CHAPTER 10

Cultural and Linguistic Diversity: Influences on Preschool Inclusion

Marci J. Hanson

MING-MING IS ONE OF HIS Montessori teacher's favorite students. He often gets to sit on his teacher's lap during story time. He appears well liked by his peers and is fully included in his preschool class, where he is the only child with special needs. However, children seldom interact with him although he often plays alongside them on a tricycle or with cars. His parents speak Cantonese at home, his preschool teachers speak English, and his classmates speak English or Spanish. At age 3, Ming-Ming does not speak nor does he have a language system.

Angelica, a young child with Down syndrome, attends a fully inclusive preschool class. Her best friend is a classmate, Jose, who rides to school each morning with her on the "special education" bus. Although she is assigned a Spanish-speaking paraprofessional and one of her teachers speaks some Spanish, most of her classmates are English-speaking. Angelica speaks only Spanish, and her verbal skills are below age level. She often watches peers at play and tries to join in. During one pretend play session in the housekeeping area, she attempted to participate in "making cookies." Two other girls made fun of the way she was rolling the dough and of her inability to join the conversation.

Both Ming-Ming and Angelica have significant disabilities. Both also come from families that are immigrants to the United States and speak a language other than English at home. Each child shows delays and differences in communication and social interaction patterns as compared with peers. Their school experiences are affected both by their disabling conditions and because their cultural background and language differ from those of the majority in their classroom.

Figures recently released from the 2000 Census estimate that one in 10 of America's residents are foreign-born ("One in 10 Foreign-born," 2001). Demographic shifts in the population of the United States also are reflected in childhood population figures. Data in 1997 revealed that approximately 66% of children were Caucasian (non-Hispanic), 15% were African American (non-Hispanic), 15% were Hispanic, 4% were Asian and Pacific Islander, and 1% were American Indian or Alaskan Native (Federal Interagency Forum on Child and Family Statistics, 1998). The number of Caucasian (non-Hispanic) children has decreased since the early 1980s, whereas the number of Hispanic children has increased significantly. The number of Asian children also has increased, but the percentages of African American and American Indian children have remained relatively the same. Many of these children were enrolled in some type of school program. Census information also tells us that 48.3% of preschool-aged children participated in school experiences. Across culturally-linguistically diverse groups, 47.9% of Caucasian children, 49.9% of African American children, and 38.1% of Hispanic children attended preschool (U.S. Census Bureau, 1998). From this information, it is clear that many young children are enrolled in preschool services and that this population of children reflects the cultural and linguistic diversity of the overall U.S. population. Many preschool-aged children now come from cultural and ethnic groups that differ from the dominant or mainstream culture.

This cultural and linguistic diversity in our country's citizenry has produced new challenges and opportunities for service delivery systems such as special education and early childhood education. These service issues include the need to train teachers in cross cultural competence, the development of curricula and materials that reflect *all* of America's children, the provision of supports and services for families from diverse backgrounds and perspectives, and the provision of translation and interpretation services, to name only a few (Bredekamp & Copple, 1997; Garcia & McLaughlin, 1995; Garcia & Malkin, 1993; Hanson, Lynch, & Wayman, 1990; Harry, 1992a, 1992b; Kagan & Garcia; 1991; Lynch & Hanson, 1993, 1998; Tabors, 1997).

The purpose of this chapter is to examine the lessons we have learned through the ECRII project about serving in inclusive settings young children who have special needs and who are *also* diverse with respect to cultural and linguistic backgrounds. The influences of children's cultural and linguistic diversity will be described with regard to children's relationships with their peers in classrooms, their families' communications and interactions with preschool systems, preschool systems' philosophies and policies, and societal and community values. Given the tremendous influence of these factors on children's access to and participation in educational services, implications for practice are provided for supporting children from many cultural and linguistic backgrounds and ability levels.

CHILDREN'S RELATIONSHIPS

In Chapter 5, we discussed the social relationships of children with disabilities and their peers. In this chapter, we look specifically at the influence of the children's cultural and linguistic backgrounds on these relationships. We studied these interactions chiefly through observations of children's experiences with their classroom peers.

Belonging and Membership in Peer Culture

One aspect of peer culture (described in Chapter 5) is the child's seeking acceptance and membership in peer interactions (Hanson et al., 1998). In our study, children who were more socially and linguistically competent tended to use *more conventional verbal and nonverbal social cues and behaviors* to initiate or enter into activities with peers, such as watching, verbally asking, showing materials, or easing into a social situation. Children with significant delays or differences in social or linguistic development tended to use *more nonconventional social-communicative strategies*. For example, Ricky, a Filipino boy with speech and language delays, resorted to physical initiations. He often used hitting or grabbing and intrusive affectionate responses (hugging and kissing) to get attention or enter peer interactions. Another example is that of Angelica, the Spanish-speaking child with Down syndrome previously discussed. She participated more passively by watching or following peers from a distance.

Another dimension of participating in peer culture came through *children discovering common ground* for interaction, for example, playing house.

> One girl says to the other, "Tu es la Mama" (You are the mother). Analuna protests, "No, es mia—soy la Mama" (No, it's mine—I'm the mother). Analuna goes to the rolling bathtub and picks up a baby doll: "Tu mi bebe, tu mi bebe" (You my baby, you my baby). The other girls take roles along side her. (Hanson et al., 1998, p. 192)

When children shared "scripts" and experiences for these play routines, they were able to participate more readily. When children did not have this background or experience, they often were unable to enter the play situation.

Thus, children whose behavior, toy preferences, role playing, or language were different from those of their peers sometimes were excluded or unable to enter into the peer culture. At times both the characteristics of the child's disability as well as the differences in cultural or linguistic background influenced their interactions.

Role of Language and Communication

The previous discussion highlights the importance of communication and language skills in peer interactions. Communication and social interaction difficulties sometimes developed for children with limited communication skills and for children who did not share a common language. In our research, we studied how culture, language, and disability worked together as a barrier to (or facilitator of) inclusion (Hanson, Gutierrez, Morgan, Brennan, & Zercher, 1997). For instance, lack of speech and language prevented Ming-Ming (mentioned at the beginning of this chapter) from fully participating in his class and interfered with his learning. When we interviewed his parents several years after he was in the preschool, we found that his limited communication skills had had a profound effect on his school experiences (Hanson et al., in press). Although Ming-Ming was fully included in preschool, when he reached kindergarten he was placed in a segregated special education class because of his lack of communication skills. He remained in noninclusive special education placements.

Speaking a language other than the majority language was also isolating to Jose and Angelica. Both children had disabilities (one with physical impairments, one with Down syndrome) and rode to school in a "special education" bus. This factor cemented their friendship but also identified them as separate or different from classmates. Because both children spoke Spanish, although English was the majority language in the classroom, they were assigned a Spanish-speaking paraprofessional to assist them in the class. The teacher spoke some Spanish, and the paraprofessional made efforts to include the children in class activities and support their native language. However, the presence of an instructional aide as well as their language differences further isolated them from others and they became a kind of subunit within the class.

Language difference, however, was not always a barrier. In classrooms where a climate of acceptance and support for differences was nurtured, friendships and communication occurred despite language differences and developmental delays. The following conversation between Lenny, an African American English-speaking boy with cerebral palsy, and Carlos, a typically developing Latino peer, demonstrates this point.

> [Lenny and Carlos] were sitting next to each other at the lunch cart, and Carlos had mangled his [empty] little paper cup . . . and he had it in his lap. And he was making it go, "Lenny, Lenny"; he was making it talk. And he told me in Spanish [it] was a talking cup. And so I knew enough to translate it for Lenny. I said, "Oh, Carlos is making a talking cup. Look what it says, 'Lenny, Lenny.'" And so Lenny mangled his cup and they kind of did that for awhile. And then they started making faces to each other. . . . And then Carlos started changing it. He'd touch his nose. And then Lenny would touch his nose. . . . They would laugh . . . and then there were a couple of kids watching them . . . it was really special because they were just having a good time with each other. (Hanson et al., 1997, pp. 321–322)

Children with disabilities who also come from cultural and linguistic backgrounds that differ from those of their classmates may experience difficulties in joining activities unless their unique needs are identified and supported. However, in classrooms where teachers anticipated these issues, children's interactions were enhanced and their inclusion was successful.

FAMILY ISSUES

Through our study we found that cultural and linguistic diversity had a great influence on families' experiences and interactions with one another and with school and program personnel. These were reflected in parents' values, family friendship and interactional patterns, parents' ability to advocate, and family choice and decision making.

Parental Values

We felt that an important finding in our research was that the values of parents of children with and without disabilities were very similar regardless of cultural or linguistic values. Most parents held *common values* with respect to their children's education and future goals and expectations. Parents often expressed the desire for their children to learn, become productive citizens, make friends, be able to get a job someday, live independently, have manners, study hard, and "be happy" (Hanson et al., 1998; Hanson et al., in press). They also held similar views with respect to inclusion. Families of children with disabilities expressed the hope that inclusion might help their children "reach their potential," "make friends," "make a productive citizen out of himself," and "get the experience he needs in relating to typically developing kids" (Hanson et al., in press). Families of children without disabilities tended to support the practice of inclusion and thought education should be the same for all children.

Cultural background, however, did sometimes influence parents' explanations of their children's disabilities (Hanson et al., 1998). For some parents, the child's disability was attributed to hereditary factors in the family, whereas for others it was explained by fate or chance. The influence of larger social-cultural influences was mentioned as well. One mother, for instance, related her concern about the overdiagnosis of attention deficit disorders in children of color.

Families' cultural background and experience also influenced their knowledge and views about inclusion (Hanson et al., 1998). For example, Ming-Ming's parents were recent immigrants from the People's Republic of China, and for them the term *inclusion* was a new concept, as were many provisions of preschool education and special education. They did not understand the special education approach of partnering with parents, nor did they know that various service model options existed for their child in preschool.

Families' cultural values also played a role in families' philosophy of preschool education. A number of families advocated more compensatory and structured educational experiences. Other families placed more value on socialization experiences and did not want a classroom with too many rules. Some families valued a program that focused on teaching manners and "appropriate" behavior, such as the one a teacher describes:

> We also [work] on cleanliness. That right there is very important . . . because we tell them to be sure and wash their hands promptly and always flush the potty. And also manners, like at the table . . . so we help them with that, and their "please" and "thank-yous" . . . those are magic words. (Hanson et al., 1998, p. 192)

At times these family perspectives were matched with teacher perspectives on the best educational experiences for young children, whereas in other instances they were at odds (Hanson et al., 1998).

The issue of primary language(s) spoken in the classroom sometimes presented challenges. Teachers were not always available to support a child in her or his primary language, although it was the family's goal to have their child participate in a bilingual educational experience. Yet, language differences were not always barriers. In fact, families of both English-speaking and non-English-speaking children were pleased that their children were learning a second language. The following comment by the mother of a Spanish-speaking typically developing peer is a humorous example of this opportunity:

> He's much happier now that he can speak English . . . he doesn't get upset. He was . . . really concerned last year that he was going to see Santa Claus, and what if Santa Claus asked him how old he was? What was he going to tell him? Because he couldn't tell him in English. And how would you say "Carlito" in English, if Santa Claus asked him his name? And how was he going to tell him what he wanted for Christmas in English? Because he couldn't speak . . . English. Where now, this year there was no problem. (Hanson et al., 1997, pp. 321–322)

Family Friendship and Interactional Patterns

Not only were children's friendships and interactional patterns influenced by cultural and linguistic diversity—so were their families' experiences in the preschool programs. The family's cultural background, language spoken, and socioeconomic status tended to play a greater role in the friendships family members developed and social networks in the program than did the child's developmental status (disabled vs. nondisabled) (Hanson et al., 1998). Although parents in general were satisfied with their experiences in preschool, they sometimes told us that they had little in common with other families in the program. This seemed particularly true in Head Start programs where income eligibility had been waived for children with disabilities from middle-class families. It also occurred sometimes in other programs when families were from different cultural and linguistic backgrounds. A single mother of a child with disabilities told us: "They're usually married families. The Spanish speaking—well I know the women stay home. Take care of the kids. And the man works. Where I have to go to work, go to school, take care of him and I don't get any help" (cited in Hanson et al., 1998, p. 201). These differences and difficulties in communication did not, however, interfere with families' participation in their children's programs.

Family Choice and Decision Making

One of the most powerful influences we found across family studies in the ECRII was the role of professional opinions in families' decisions and choices (Hanson et al., 2000; Hanson et al., in press; Hanson et al., 1998). Although families differed in their views on the importance of professionals in decision making regarding children's services, cultural perspectives exerted a major influence in this area. In some cultures, professional opinions were less likely to be questioned, and the authority figures received great respect and deference to their judgments. In other cultural groups, families took a more independent stance.

For some families, the issue was not so much cultural perspective as an issue of power and access to information. Families who were English-speaking and better educated tended to have greater access to information and support and often played a more active role in their children's educational programs. These parents were described by one director as "savvy," and they were more likely to procure desired services, as the following quotation from a mother illustrates:

> We essentially got an IEP and I know, I know how to work with it . . . which is half the battle. . . . We were able to argue successfully to keep him out of kindergarten this year . . . we just said, he is not ready. . . . We have arranged for Gary to be in a mainstreamed [kindergarten] classroom [next year]. We've been able to get the teacher we want for him. He will continue to get occupa-

tional and speech therapy and he'll continue to work with [his present speech therapist]. (Hanson et al., 1998, p. 203)

A program consultant in one large school district added:

> They especially welcome white middle class or upper middle class families because they know those people have the time and energy to put back into the schools and that kind of thing. That those are the people that know how. The families that are not as informed or from a different cultural system—whatever—those kids are not going to be high on the totem pole and maybe never will be fully included because . . . there's so many others in the pecking order. (Hanson et al., 1998, p. 204)

She explained how family advocacy was necessary in that district to "make sure you get your papers in, meet your deadlines, talk to the right people at the right time" (Hanson et al., 1998). Thus, parents who were familiar with special education systems and jargon and who had the ability to advocate for their children were more likely to participate in decisions relating to their children's educational experiences. On the other hand, families who came from cultures other than the mainstream and who spoke languages other than English often were less involved in choices and decision making. Thus, the roles families played in their children's educational programs and in making decisions varied greatly and were strongly influenced by their access to information and the supports they received. Language, culture, education, and economic differences were key variables that influenced families' abilities to procure this information and support.

PRESCHOOL SYSTEMS

Programs differed in their philosophy regarding and support for diversity. Observations and interviews revealed a number of examples of adaptations or accommodations that teachers and programs made to children's unique characteristics and needs (Hanson et al., 1998).

Programs in which diversity was cherished appeared to have a spirit of inclusion for all children, including those with disabilities. Issues of culture were evident, though, even in these programs. For instance, in one classroom in which personnel prided themselves on cultural competence and diversity, the mother of one of the children expressed her surprise that her daughter's name was Anglicized rather than spoken with its Spanish pronunciation.

In many classes teachers went to great lengths to demonstrate their respect for and support of families' preferences. An example was one classroom's birthday celebration for a teacher. The family of one of the children were members of the Jehovah Witness faith that refrains from the celebration of birthdays. During the birthday party, the child, Gisela, was given an alternative activity. Gisela's mother expressed her appreciation for this support for her family's beliefs.

> They [Head Start] respect a lot our belief because the other day, I came to the school and Gisela said, "Mommy, look at what Rita gave me," and I said why, [and she said] because I was with Rita and [I asked] why you were with Rita, you are supposed to be here. And [her] teacher say, because we were celebrating teacher Margarita's birthday, and we don't celebrate birthdays [so Gisela spent special time with Rita]. (Hanson et al., 1998, p. 202)

This was one of many occasions on which we witnessed staff members' respect and accommodations for various cultural and/or religious practices (Hanson et al., 1998).

SOCIETAL VALUES

The philosophical and cultural values of the larger society or community in which programs were located also affected the inclusion of children with a wide variety of abilities and backgrounds (Hanson et al., 1998).

Valuing Diversity

In our research, we interviewed policy makers and administrators to determine their goals and priorities. We also reviewed characteristics of communities and educational districts as well as school policy and mission statements. Some communities placed a high value on the inclusion of *all* children in their school programs. As the special education administrator in one community related:

> You're in a community that is very aware of their rights . . . the parents are very knowledgeable—and rightly so—and they're wonderful advocates for their children . . . if something is going to happen, it always happens [here] first . . . this has always been a community that feels that what kids need they should get. (Hanson et al., 1998, pp. 202–203)

Another administrator demonstrated the impact of this commitment as well. She stated: "We seek to create a community in which all of us have a place and are valued" (Hanson et al., 1998, p. 204). She worked hard to transform these principles into practice through a program that merged child care and special education services and a community playground on her school campus in order to provide services to all the children of the very diverse community in all their diversity.

Access to Inclusive Educational Services

Although the least-restrictive educational placements have been stipulated by legal and regulatory actions for some time, inclusion options were more openly communicated as an option in some communities than in others (Hanson et al., 2000; Hanson et al., in press; Hanson et al., 1998). In some communities and school systems, administrators actively recruited children for inclusive placements and expanded service options, while administrators in other programs did not begin with inclusion as an option unless the family openly advocated for it. For some children, placement was linked to a personal contact and their linguistic background. For instance, Jorge, a preschooler with autism, was referred to a local Head Start program by a neighbor who happened to work as an educational assistant in the program. Because Jorge's family spoke Spanish and other Spanish-speaking services were not available in the community, the school district approved his placement in the Head Start program.

In summary, children entered inclusive programs through many different paths, but the issues of the family's language and socioeconomic status played a role. A key influence was the larger social-political climate or philosophy of the community and the values adopted and practiced by the educational community with respect to diversity and inclusion.

IMPLICATIONS FOR PRACTICE

The cultural and linguistic background of children and their families exerts a major influence on children's access to and participation in educational services. Diversity among children presents challenges for educational services as well as opportunities for valuable learning experiences. The recommendations that follow are aimed at highlighting the importance of cultural/linguistic diversity and fostering services to support children from many backgrounds and ability levels.

Providing Culturally Sensitive Services

Many leaders in the field identify the need for culturally respectful and responsive services for young children and their families (for instance, Anderson & Fenichel, 1989; Barrera, 2000; Bredekamp & Copple, 1997; Lynch & Hanson, 1998; Okagaki & Diamond, 2000). While teachers and directors in most programs are aware of the diverse needs of children and families, they may still require additional information and organizational and policy shifts to meet the needs of children from such diverse backgrounds.

These challenges may be particularly keen when children with diverse abilities requiring special education are included in early education programs and when these children also come from a variety of cultural or linguistic groups. Language difference and disability may work together to compound service delivery challenges (Hanson et al., 1998).

Training. A primary concern is to provide early childhood staff members with an awareness of the teaching issues and the skills to work with children who vary with respect to ability levels and cultural/linguistic background. Children with disabilities also need services from other professionals who must have training in their area of specialization (e.g., special education, physical or occupational therapy, speech and language therapy), as well as the ability to work in a culturally sensitive and family-centered manner. Thus, training in this area remains crucial to successful inclusion experiences. It is not enough for programs to merely have materials, days, or events that represent different cultural perspectives (e.g., sampling foods from a variety of cultures). Rather, teachers must learn about the values and belief systems, meanings of words and gestures, styles of communication, and styles of information exchange of children and families who have a variety of perspectives, and those different perspectives must be reflected and honored in the classroom.

Parents often told us that they wanted their children's teachers to be competent and knowledgeable about the children's disabilities as well as able to communicate with the children in their native languages. Staff members, too, spoke of the challenges of serving the diverse needs of children as well as their own growth when they acquired new skills. The following statement by a Head Start teacher after her first year of experience with an inclusive bilingual classroom reflects these teaching issues:

> If you're a teacher . . . there's so much to learn. The world is so diverse and there's so much. And it opens up a whole new world. Just like this past year. I've learned so much. I've learned more Spanish. I can communicate

with Spanish people. I mean, you know, at the beginning of the year, I . . . could barely spit anything out. And at the end of the year I was able to carry on a conversation. And I got to know these families and they're really nice . . . if I would just limit myself, gosh, . . . I'd lose out on so much. (Hanson et al., 1997, p. 333)

Meeting Children's Learning Needs

Our work suggests that while preschool programs typically provide wonderful avenues for socialization and learning, children's educational goals are not always addressed fully. We found that children's individualized education programs did not always include identified or defined goals with respect to their language. Procedures for communication assistance and the language in which the services were to be delivered were lacking in some instances (Hanson et al., 1997). Ming-Ming's experience exemplifies this issue. Different languages were spoken in his home and school, and he was not provided with specific services for acquiring a language system. His parents identified speech and language as a major goal for him, and school personnel agreed. However, the only speech and language therapist for his preschool class spoke English and Spanish (as did his teachers). This cultural gap resulted in the lack of services for this child. Because Ming-Ming was not given help in acquiring speech and language in his early years, he went to kindergarten without any speech or language system. At that point he was unable to continue in an inclusive class placement, and he was placed in segregated special education services due to his severe developmental delays, particularly in language. The system failed this child.

Services in the child's native language. Many children in our study experienced difficulties or failed to have their service goals delivered due to the lack of personnel who spoke their language. Interpretation and translation services are vital to the provision of services to children and families from non-English-speaking backgrounds. As the example of Ming-Ming suggests, given today's diverse population of children, issues of language must be addressed in preschool programs and support must be given to children and their families.

Communication between peers and with families. Interactions between children sometimes were influenced by the children's inability to understand one another or speak the same language. This happened for family / school partnerships as well. When families were not provided information in a format and language that they could understand, they were unable to fully communicate with other parents and teachers, or otherwise to participate in a meaningful manner (Hanson et al., 1997). Again, interpretation and translation services are essential for this communication. For a fully family-centered approach, these language supports must be given.

Valuing Diversity: The Influence of Philosophy

Although differences in culture and language background can function as barriers to interactions and effective communication, they need not. We found that when programs held an underlying and abiding commitment to supporting diversity and facilitating interactions, they were able to achieve those goals. Thus, starting with a mission statement and actively supporting children and families from diverse backgrounds and abilities is an essential beginning step.

Coordinating Service Systems

Children with special needs and children from non-English-speaking backgrounds and nondominant cultures often receive services through a variety of agencies. These services are paid for by different funding sources that have different regulations and eligibility requirements. Additionally, the personnel providing these services come from professional backgrounds that differ with respect to type of degree, length of training, training requirements, and salary. Further, few training programs are interdisciplinary or require skills for working with teams of professionals.

To provide successful inclusive programs for children, our research has shown that it is essential for these administrative systems and personnel to work together. When they work separately in an uncoordinated way, they act as barriers to appropriate service. Children's and families' needs cannot be parceled out. In those programs that advocated and allowed adequate planning time for staff members as well as integrated, coordinated service systems (early education, special education, bilingual education), children's and families' needs were more likely to be met.

Providing Family Support and Services

A great deal has been written about the importance of family-centered and culturally responsive programs for young children and their families. It is unlikely that a program can be culturally responsive and culturally sensitive without being family-centered, nor can services be considered family-centered if they are not respectful and sensitive to a family's cultural beliefs, values, and language. In our work, we witnessed a number of instances where families were limited in their participation due to the language they spoke, their cultural background, and/or their socioeconomic status. We also witnessed fine examples of programs that recognized the importance of meaningful and respectful family participation. When programs identified this as a major goal, provided ongoing training to staff members about this type of family support, used the families' native languages, and respected the families' values and beliefs, families typically were able to become active members and participants on their children's educational teams. We found that even a single program director or teacher could change services for the better through advocacy and support to families.

CONCLUSION

The increasing diversity of children and families enrolled in our educational programs adds wonderful opportunities for growth for staff members. Teachers and other professionals have the opportunity to learn about new ideas, cultures, words, language systems, and lifestyles. The inclusion of children with differing abilities also provides new opportunities for educators to hone their skills and acquire new levels of information and better teaching techniques. This diversity of children and families in educational programs brings with it not only these avenues for growth but also challenges. We have observed many excited and effective teachers and administrators who met this challenge and became leaders for change. An open mind and an open heart appeared to be essential to fully achieving these goals. We welcome readers to strive to ensure that *all* children and their families are included in programs and given appropriate and meaningful experiences.

The following story embodies the challenges and opportunities available to early educators when they serve children and their families from a wide variety of backgrounds. It was told by a school principal who was one of the most resourceful, effective, and caring professionals we met.

This is just a little story that kind of illustrates the levels at which this impacts people. We had one of our parents come to me and say, "I don't want my child eating with this other child." It happened to be an Asian parent—immigrant parent—talking about her child eating with a child who had Down syndrome. And I said, then you don't want your child at this center, because that's what we do. It's really important to us. And I'd feel terrible if your child left the center, but I can't separate the two groups of children because one of the things that's very important to us is to educate the heart as well as the head and that's what we want for all our children. And then she was kind of troubled and I just asked her if she would do me a favor and come to lunch one day so she could see what happens when the children are mixed. So she came to lunch and . . . she came to me afterwards, and I'm pretty sure she had tears in her eyes, and she told me it was all right. I mean, you know, that's really powerful stuff.

But it all seems to us that everything flows from what our ethical underpinnings are. So that what we want to do is really look at what are the values that we hold dear and that we want for our children. And that the curriculum should flow from those values. . . . That there's much more to teach children and in that context of that body of knowledge, all those other things, like circles and squares can come, but the real key is what do we really believe? What do we hold to be really sacred about life and about what we want for kids? . . . And the idea is that all of us together want to come up with a curriculum that is really site-based, that flows from our sense of importance of diversity, importance of building community and seeing the child in the context of the community. (in Hanson et al., 1998, pp. 206–208)

REFERENCES

Anderson, P. P., & Fenichel, E. S. (1989). *Serving culturally diverse families of infants and toddlers with disabilities.* Washington, DC: National Center for Clinical Infant Programs.

Barrera, I. (2000). Honoring differences: Essential features of appropriate ECSE services for young children from diverse sociocultural environments. *Young Exceptional Children, 3*(4), 17–24.

Bredekamp, S., & Copple, C. (Eds.). (1997). *Developmentally appropriate practice in early childhood programs* (rev. ed.). Washington, DC: National Association for the Education of Young Children.

Federal Interagency Forum on Child and Family Statistics. (1998). *America's children: Key national indicators of well-being.* Washington, DC: U.S. Government Printing Office.

Garcia, E. E., & McLaughlin, B., with Spodek, B., & Saracho, O. N. (Eds.). (1995). *Yearbook in Early Childhood Education: Vol. 6. Meeting the challenge of linguistic and cultural diversity in early childhood education.* New York: Teachers College Press.

Garcia, S. B., & Malkin, D. H. (1993). Toward defining programs and services for culturally and linguistically diverse learners in special education. *Teaching Exceptional Children, 26*(1), 52–58.

Hanson, M. J., Beckman, P., Horn, E., Marquart, J., Sandall, S., Greig, D., & Brennan, E. (2000). Entering preschool: Family and professional experiences in this transition process. *Journal of Early Intervention, 23,* 279–293.

Hanson, M. J., Gutierrez, S., Morgan, M., Brennan, E., & Zercher, C. (1997). Language, culture, and disability: Interacting influences on preschool inclusion. *Topics in Early Childhood Special Education, 17*(3), 307–336.

Hanson, M. J., Horn, E., Sandall, S., Beckman, P., Morgan, M., Marquart, J., Barnwell, D., & Chou, H-Y. (in press). After preschool inclusion: Children's educational pathways over the early school years. *Exceptional Children*.

Hanson, M. J., Lynch, E. W., & Wayman, K. I. (1990). Honoring the cultural diversity of families when gathering data. *Topics in Early Childhood Special Education, 10* (1), 112–131.

Hanson, M. J., Wolfberg, P., Zercher, C., Morgan, M., Gutierrez, S., Barnwell, D., & Beckman, P. J. (1998). The culture of inclusion: Recognizing diversity at multiple levels. *Early Childhood Research Quarterly, 13*(1), 185–209.

Harry, B. (1992a). *Cultural diversity, families, and the special education system: Communication and empowerment.* New York: Teachers College Press.

Harry, B. (1992b). Developing cultural awareness: The first step in values clarification for early interventionists. *Topics in Early Childhood Special Education, 12,* 333–350.

Kagan, S., & Garcia, E. (1991). Education of culturally and linguistically diverse preschoolers: Moving the agenda. *Early Childhood Research Quarterly, 6,* 427–443.

Lynch, E. W., & Hanson, M. J. (1993). Changing demographics: Implications for early intervention. *Infants and Young Children, 6*(1), 50–55.

Lynch, E. W., & Hanson, M. J. (1998). *Developing cross-cultural competence: A guide for working with children and their families* (2nd ed.). Baltimore, MD: Brookes.

Okagaki, L., & Diamond, K. E. (2000). Responding to cultural and linguistic differences in the beliefs and practices of families of young children. *Young Children, 55*(3), 74–80.

One in 10 foreign-born, new figures estimate. (2001, January 3). *San Jose Mercury News,* p. 9A.

Tabors, P. O. (1997). *One child, two languages: A guide for preschool educators of children learning English as a second language.* Baltimore, MD: Brookes.

U.S. Census Bureau (1998). School enrollment of the population. http://www.census.gov/population/estimates/socdemo/school/report96/taba-1.txt

So What Do We Know from All This? Synthesis Points of Research on Preschool Inclusion

Samuel L. Odom, Ilene S. Schwartz,
& ECRII Investigators

AT THE MIDPOINT OF OUR RESEARCH PROJECT on preschool inclusion, we met with our advisory board, comprising researchers, professors, and parents, to help us plan ways to best share our findings with the field. We had completed our ecological systems study and follow up studies with parents and programs, and we were completing studies testing teaching approaches, collaboration approaches, and ways of working with families. As we presented descriptions of these studies and our findings, both our advisory board and our entire research team were overwhelmed with the amount of our data. During the ensuing discussion, one insightful member of our board proposed that we summarize our research findings in a way that would enable anyone to learn quickly about our findings.

We took this task to heart. At our next investigators' meeting, we decided to establish a set of "synthesis points" to represent themes reflected in the findings across studies. Our goal was to create no more than eight points, and to use no more than eight words describing each point. Over the next several months, we reviewed our completed research, identified themes, stated, revised, restated, and revised again until we all agreed on a final set of points that reflected the identified themes. Although our word limit was exceeded on a few points, we were satisfied that the set of points conveyed the central findings of our work. These synthesis points are listed in Table 11.1 (Early Childhood Research Institute on Inclusion, 1998; Schwartz, Odom, & Sandall, 1999). In this concluding chapter, we describe these points, briefly identify how they are supported by our research, and propose implications of the points for practice.

INCLUSION IS ABOUT BELONGING AND PARTICIPATING IN A DIVERSE SOCIETY

Our research began in inclusive preschool classes. Yet, as we talked with parents and teachers, observed in classrooms, and stepped into communities, we became aware that while inclusion is very much about being a part of the class, it also goes beyond the four walls of the class and reflects families' and children's experiences with the school system and community. Also, we found that inclusion is more than a disability issue; it relates to the need for all children to be a part of the classroom.

1. *Inclusion is about belonging and participating in a diverse society.* Inclusion is not just a school issue—it extends to the communities in which children and their families live. Inclusion is not only a disability issue; all children have a right to participate and be supported in the schools and community.

2. *Individuals—teachers, families, administrators—define inclusion differently.* Levels of the ecological system, priorities, and responsibilities influence definitions of inclusion. People within the same system (e.g., one school or school district) may have extremely different views of inclusion.

3. *Beliefs about inclusion influence its implementation.* The beliefs about schooling that families and professionals bring with them to the classroom influence how inclusive practices are planned and implemented; these beliefs are influenced by many complex factors. Beliefs about human diversity—culture, race, language, class, ability—influence how inclusion is implemented in schools and communities.

4. *Programs, not children, have to be "ready for inclusion."* The most successful inclusive programs view inclusion as the starting point for all children. Inclusion can be appropriate for all children; making it work successfully depends on planning, training, and support.

5. *Collaboration is the cornerstone of effective inclusive programs.* Collaboration among adults, including professionals and parents, within and across systems and programs is essential to inclusive programs. Collaboration among adults, from different disciplines and often with different philosophies, is one of the greatest challenges to successful implementation of inclusive programs.

6. *Specialized instruction is an important component of inclusion.* Participation in a community-based or general education setting is not enough. The individual needs of children with disabilities must be addressed in inclusive programs. Specialized instruction can be delivered through a variety of effective strategies, many of which can be embedded in the ongoing classroom activities.

7. *Adequate support is necessary to make inclusive environments work.* Support includes training, personnel, materials, planning time, and ongoing consultation. Support can be delivered in different ways, and each person involved in inclusion may have unique needs.

8. *Inclusion can benefit children with and without disabilities.* High-quality early childhood programs form the necessary structural base for high-quality inclusive programs; thus, all children benefit from them. The parents of children without disabilities whose children participate in inclusive programs often report beneficial changes in their children's confidence, self-esteem, and understanding of diversity.

Figure 11.1. Synthesis points of the Early Childhood Research Institute on Inclusion.

Being a Member of the Class

In their research on inclusion of children with severe disabilities in elementary school classrooms, Schwartz, Peck, and colleagues (Billingsley, Gallucci, Peck, Schwartz, & Staub, 1996) identified "membership" as an important goal supported in classrooms. Membership, they found, involved both participating and being accepted in the class. Our research on child participation (described in Chapter 3) reflected the degree to which children participated as members of the class. In fact, teachers and parents told us how important membership was for children. For example, Jorge is a child identified as having autism/pervasive developmental disorder and is enrolled in the Santa Luna Head Start program in the afternoon and a special education class in the morning. His mother told us "that in the Head Start program, they treat him like any other child. . . . [After the special education class] he comes to Head Start and it's not like therapy. It is a regular class and he has a chance to socialize with other kids" (Wolfberg, Hanson, & Zercher, 1995, p. 51).

Our CASPER observations, described in Chapter 3, also revealed the extent to which children were members of the class. Indeed, our data revealed that overall, children with disabilities were involved in groups with typically developing peers more often than they were involved in solitary activities or group activities with only children with disabilities. Furthermore, the children with disabilities were actively engaged in the activities as often as typically developing peers. Unfortunately, however, our studies also revealed that membership was limited for some children with disabilities. We observed instances of social rejection (see Chapter 5), which may well have influenced children's membership in the class.

Being a Member of the Community

In Chapters 7 and 8, we described the experiences of families and the various factors that limited both families' and children's participation in the community and support community participation. We found that some parents expressed a strong preference for having their child with disabilities in a nearby child care program or neighborhood school, rather than having their child bused to another part of town. Shelly, for example, was an African American child with visual impairments receiving services through the VIP program (Horn, Odom, Marquart, Pallas, & Kaiser, 1995). It was important to her parents that she attend the Power Kids Child Care program, which was close to their home. Although this program did not meet traditional ideas of quality (e.g., children were in adult-initiated activities nearly all day and spent a large amount of time sitting at tables), we understood that it very much reflected the African American culture of the community. Shelly was actively involved as a member of the class, and, importantly, other children from her neighborhood attended the program.

Implications for Practice

- Teachers should plan class activities in ways that support the membership of all children in the class.
- Teachers should recognize that families may have priorities for membership that extend outside the classroom, and those priorities should be supported whenever possible.
- Teachers should recognize that disability is one of many possible diverse characteristics of children in inclusive preschool classes. Thus, planning a classroom environment that addresses the diverse needs of all children is important.

INDIVIDUALS—TEACHERS, FAMILIES, ADMINISTRATORS— DEFINE INCLUSION DIFFERENTLY

In Chapter 2, we described how different programs defined inclusion differently. Across the levels of the ecology in which inclusive programs are embedded, individuals often hold different meanings of inclusion— for parents, inclusion may have one meaning; for teachers, perhaps another meaning; and perhaps an even different meaning for administrators or policy makers. We previously described Shelly's inclusive placement. For her parents, inclusion meant that Shelly would participate in a program close to her home and with members of the community. Their definition was based on the value they placed on having Shelly be a member of the class and community. Shelly's itinerant teachers, and we as researchers, however, defined inclusion with a more educational orientation, and we based our judgment of her inclusive setting on the traditional indicators of quality of an early childhood environment.

Another example of differences in definition occurred when we began initial recruitment for programs. We started by asking program administrators for their definition of inclusion. Administrators at the Winwood program identified classrooms that were following an integrative-activities model in which children with disabilities were together most of the day, but at some time during the day joined a classroom of children without disabilities for joint activities. Although both administrators and teachers agreed that this model was inclusive, it differed from the federal government's definition, which classifies inclusion as 79% of a child's day being spent in the regular classroom (U.S. Department of Education, 1999). Likewise, the definition of inclusion held by these administrators and teachers differed from the perspectives of professional organizations in the early childhood special education field (Division for Early Childhood, 2000).

Differences in the definition of inclusion also may be found among individuals within a system. Sometimes, these differences lead to conflicts, and sometimes they lead to a stronger system. In the Beacon Street program, the team teaching model was used to define the program as inclusive. Within the system, however, administrators were open to other definitions or models. One system-level administrator defined inclusion by describing an alternative model that was under consideration.

> We are going to have an Early Environment Teacher who travels to the Head Start centers where it is appropriate for those children to remain in Head Start but to get their special education instruction in that Head Start class. (Lieber, Beckman, Li, Herring, & Barnwell, 1996, p. 42)

Implications for Practice

- Teachers and individuals within school systems must be aware of the different meanings that parents have for inclusion, and how those meanings relate to the goals that parents have for their children.
- Administrators, teachers, other practitioners, and parents should work toward a commonly agreed-on definition of inclusion and the goals that may be associated with that definition.
- A useful way of establishing a commonly agreed-on definition of inclusion is to develop a mission statement for the inclusive program (for an example, see Wolery & Odom, 2000, p. 85).

BELIEFS ABOUT INCLUSION INFLUENCE ITS IMPLEMENTATION

Beliefs about inclusion go beyond holding a philosophical position; they directly influence actions of teachers in classrooms. Research on teacher beliefs conducted by other researchers (Clark & Peterson, 1986) support this point, and we found similar outcomes in our research (Lieber et al., 1998). In the Wesley Child Care Center (a community-based inclusive classroom that was part of the VIP program), administrators held the professional belief that their program should be child-directed, and Wesley teachers stated that their goals were to support child initiation or selection of activities. Our CASPER data confirmed that more child-initiated activity occurred in this classroom than any other we observed. For Kevin, the children with Down syndrome in this program, it meant that to be included, he had to learn to make choices, stay in an activity, and participate.

Conversely, teachers in the Beacon Street program, where a team teaching model was followed, believed that inclusion meant children with disabilities and typically developing children were treated the same. So, as mentioned in Chapter 4, when we attempted to conduct research on modifying activities to accommodate the needs of children with disabilities, and on embedding learning opportunities in ongoing classroom routines, Beacon Street teachers resisted the idea of individualizing instructional plans. In both programs, teachers' beliefs about teaching practices influenced the experiences of the children with disabilities in their classrooms.

Individual beliefs about human diversity—culture, race, language, class, and ability—also influence how inclusion is implemented in schools and communities. In some of the programs in our study, the community consisted of families from diverse cultures, which led to diversity within classrooms. Thus, including children with special needs sometimes merged with a general belief in serving children and families from different backgrounds. A social services coordinator from the Santa Luna Head Start program expressed such a belief when she told us:

> Children in my class are very diverse. The families are also diverse and I find it very challenging for these children and families because they have really different needs, special needs actually. . . . Any one of these boys is necessarily a special needs child. In fact, every child [has] special needs. (Hanson et al., 1998, p. 195)

Implications for Practice

- Teachers, family members, and administrators should express their beliefs about inclusion. Sharing expectations, ideas, and goals for children in inclusive settings is an important first step in planning programs.
- Recognition of diversity as extending beyond the issues of culture or disability is an important value and can be a centerpiece of inclusive programs.

- Celebration of differences can be a theme that fuels early childhood programs, and inclusion can become one dimension of this theme.

PROGRAMS, NOT CHILDREN, HAVE TO BE "READY FOR INCLUSION"

Chapter 8 described our study of how inclusion was maintained in various programs from our ecological systems study, and identified programs that were most successful in expanding and continuing to provide a high quality of inclusive services. A characteristic of those successful programs was their assumption that the program must be shaped to meet the needs of young children with disabilities, rather than the children having to meet specific entry criteria before they could enroll in the program—sometimes known as "earning their way into inclusive programs." We found that viewing inclusion as the starting place for planning services for children and families was a commonly held assumption. In the Lincoln County program, for example, state guidelines specified:

> Preschool programs are designed to include and meet the needs of children across a wide range of abilities in a mainstream setting. Programs . . . for 4-year-old children must provide adaptations for children with special needs. (Marquart & Tabor, 1998, p. 5)

The Director of Preschool Programs for Lincoln County told us:

> The goal of the [state-funded] preschool programs is to make sure that children are serviced, mainstreamed into typical classrooms. So, we didn't even consider another model and probably wouldn't ever, I mean it was never an issue. (p. 6)

Although our study began before the reauthorization of the current version of the Individuals with Disabilities Education Act (IDEA), we found that the successful programs held to the fundamental operating principles reflected in current law. A common value that related to the readiness of these programs to accept children with disabilities was their belief in meeting a child's individual needs in the context of an inclusive placement. One program administrator told us: "We have been instructed by our legal department to carefully look at the least restrictive environment options for the kids and to justify why we can't provide services in less restrictive settings" (Wolery & Odom, 2000, p. 13).

The assumption of "program rather than child readiness" carries with it the implication that inclusive programs are appropriate for all children.

Embedded in this assumption, however, is the assumption of sufficient planning, training, and support so the program can adequately meet the individual needs of all children. As the VIP program evolved over the years of our research, program staff found it necessary to establish different types of inclusive options in order to meet the needs of children with substantial disabilities. To provide inclusive services for children with substantial behavior problems, for example, the VIP program expanded its options from a community-based model to a team teaching model. Although driven by the need for sufficient planning, training, and support, these changes did not completely eliminate preschool special education classrooms in the district. In fact, none of the initial 16 programs in our study (except the Mayberry classroom, which was operating in a very small district) did away with all their early childhood special education classrooms. For a small percentage of children, placement in a noninte-grated special education class sometimes may be necessary to meet their specific needs. Likewise, some parents may feel strongly that their child should be in a noninclusive setting. However, in our observations of "successful" programs, this seemed to be the exception rather than the rule.

Implications for Practice

- In conforming to the current version of IDEA, school systems should begin with inclusion as a placement assumption and determine the supports necessary in order for a child with disabilities to be successful.
- Programs should not have a formal or informal policy that children with disabilities have to "earn their way into inclusive settings." That is, prerequisites for placement in inclusive settings should not be established for children with disabilities.
- Decisions about placements and services should be made on an individual basis, with the needs of the child and the concerns and priorities of the parents being primary determinants of the placement.

COLLABORATION IS THE CORNERSTONE OF
EFFECTIVE INCLUSIVE PROGRAMS

In our quest to discover the important barriers to preschool inclusion, we began looking in the classroom, assuming that the ways teachers ran their classrooms, the ways they interacted with children, or the ways children interacted with one another might present the greatest barriers to successful inclusion. Although these barriers did exist, we learned early that the greatest barriers were the interactions that occur among adults. These influences, it seemed, often occurred outside the classroom in the relationships that developed between teachers and parents, and between teachers and other professionals.

One set of collaborations we discovered were those occurring between children's programs and their families. (See Chapter 7 for a discussion of the general findings from our family research.) Some of the programs and professionals in our study collaborated very well with families of children with and children without disabilities. Not all programs and professionals, however, collaborated effectively. Our interviews with parents illustrate both the positive and negative instances of collaborations between families and professionals. The father of a Chinese child who was typically developing and enrolled in the Santa Luna program gave a positive example of collaboration. Simon's father told us: "All Head Start programs have a fair together with exhibits. . . . There are many information booths there for parents to get information about how to communicate with your child, get to know health issues, and that's useful" (Wolfberg, Hanson, & Zercher, 1995, pp. 91–92). Another example of positive collaboration came from the father of Eddie (a boy with developmental delays enrolled in the Beacon Street program), who described the importance he and his wife placed on communication with the teacher: "When I dropped him off in the morning, I say, 'How's Eddie doing?' and 'What else could I do to help him begin to read?' The father went on to report several suggestions that were made by the teacher" (Lieber, Beckman, Li, Haring, & Barnwell, 1996, pp. 114–115). Not all positive communication, however, was delivered in face-to-face interactions. Each day the teacher in Kevin's (the child with Down syndrome enrolled in the Wesley Center class of the VIP program) classroom wrote a note to his mother describing his activity during the day. Kevin's mother, along with all the other parents in the Wesley Center, had a constant flow of information from the classroom (Horn et al., 1995).

Other collaborations that contribute to the success of the classroom are those that exist between teachers and other professionals who work in the class. In Chapter 6, we discussed the importance of these collaborative relationships and suggested ways of establishing and supporting positive relationships (Lieber et al., 1997). In the Lincoln County program, which followed a community-based/itinerant teaching model, collaboration was a high priority. An itinerant teacher in that program stated:

I feel that in order to make real change occur, I have to first establish rapport with the teachers and understand where they're coming from, their needs, and show empathy. . . . So communication is a key and often times it is a problem because I interrupt [the class]. . . . But at some time you have to communicate so you just try to do it at the best time. (Marquart & Tabor, 1998, p. 27)

The early childhood teacher in the class said of this itinerant teacher:

Mrs. Simpson [the itinerant teacher] asks your input, she shares what she's doing and how she feels about things. I'd have to say she's great, she keeps us informed on what's going on with the child and asks for our input and then gives us helpful hints as far as what to do. (p. 27)

The collaboration between public schools and Head Start offers both positive and negative examples of this process. In the Vista Valley program, the local school system and the Head Start program spent several years working out an arrangement for children with disabilities to be placed in the Head Start centers and receive support from an itinerant teacher who often moved into a co-teaching role in the classroom. This collaborative relationship evolved over time.

In contrast, the Winter County classroom of the Northumberland program, operating in its first year, was confronted with logistical, philosophical, and interpersonal issues existing between the organizations. These issues made collaboration between the Head Start and public school teachers and staff initially very difficult and eventually nearly impossible. Unfortunately, the classroom did not continue after the first year.

Implications for Practice

- Adults (professionals working in program) should establish an active working relationship with parents. One primary way of creating this relationship is to ensure that an ongoing flow of communication occurs between teachers and family members.
- Program providers should identify ways their program can respond to family needs (e.g., for information) outside traditional classroom settings (e.g., the "information fair" mentioned previously).
- Adults must realize that collaboration is a "make or break" issue for inclusive programs and work toward establishing a collaborative relationship early in the program. Such collaboration would involve open and effective modes of communication, working out philosophical differences, and other strategies identified in Chapter 6.

SPECIALIZED INSTRUCTION IS AN IMPORTANT
COMPONENT OF INCLUSION

A cornerstone of early childhood special education is the establishment of educational goals and objectives related to learning and development for children with special needs (Sandall, McLean, & Smith, 2000). We also share this value with the field of early childhood education for children who are typically developing (Bredekamp & Copple, 1997). A common assumption in early childhood special education is that for children with special needs, placement and participation in a developmentally appropriate early childhood setting is necessary but may not be sufficient for addressing individual educational objectives (Carta, Schwartz, Atwater, & McConnell, 1991; Wolery, Strain, & Bailey, 1992). In the research described in this book, we found that children with disabilities (as a group) did participate in inclusive settings, but for many children individualized instruction directed specifically toward meeting educational objectives was important.

Programs in our study varied considerably in the way they provided individual instruction. As we already have described, some programs provided services through an itinerant teacher or related service provider (e.g., speech pathologist). In those programs, the specialized professional either would work with the child with disabilities in the inclusive classroom setting or would collaborate/consult with the teacher to design ways for the child to have the needed learning opportunities in the regular curriculum. Other programs provided specialized instruction by having an early childhood education teacher and special education teacher share the role of team teachers, while still others employed a special education or "reverse mainstreaming" teacher model in which a special education teacher was the lead teacher in the class. Last, in some programs, the early childhood teacher led the program, and there was little occurring with special education teachers or other related service professionals, and little formal specialized instruction (Odom et al., 1999). As a group, we see the planning and provision of specialized instruction as a critical aspect of the quality of inclusive programs (Chapter 2), and programs with which we worked varied along this dimension of quality.

Specialized instruction does not necessarily mean that the teacher takes a child aside to a separate area and works with him or her individually for a period of time, although this may happen for some children. Specialized instruction may originate in the adaptations and modifications that teachers make in the classroom environment to allow children to participate in classroom activities. In focus groups (described in Chapter 4), teachers and other professionals have identified many ways in which they make such accommodations for children (Sandall et al., in press). In addition, important learning experiences can be embedded in ongoing activities and routines occurring in inclusive classrooms. A number of different strategies called "naturalistic interventions" have been identified (Rule, Losardo, Dinnebeil, Kaiser, & Rowland, 1998). These techniques appear under different names, such as incidental teaching (Hart & Risley, 1968), enhanced milieu training (Kaiser & Hester, 1994), activity-based instruction (Bricker, Pretti-Frontczak, & McComas, 1998), pivotal response training (Koegel, Koegel, Harrower, & Carter, 1999), and (one that our research has added to this set of approaches) embedded learning opportunities (Horn, Lieber, Sandall, Schwartz, & Shouming, 2000). All of these approaches focus on educational objectives of individual children, require the teacher to identify learning opportunities that occur in the natural setting, and provide support for practicing the skill to be learned in such settings. In Chapter 4, we describe *Building Blocks*, a set of materials based on our research, which is designed to support children's learning in inclusive settings (through specialized instruction).

Implications for Practice

- Program providers should select a model of inclusion that allows children with disabilities to receive specialized instruction.
- Specialized instruction may range from providing classroom accommodations or modifications, to individualized sessions with a student, but the critical feature is that it focuses on children's individualized educational objectives.
- Many educational objectives for students may be met through systematic use of a naturalistic teaching approach, and different naturalistic teaching strategies are available to teachers.

ADEQUATE SUPPORT IS NECESSARY TO MAKE INCLUSIVE ENVIRONMENTS WORK

By support at the classroom level, we mean the funding, training, personnel, and administrative encouragement that teachers and program providers need to set up and operate inclusive classrooms in the community, Head Start, or public schools. In Chapter 9, we described the influences that allowed school systems to provide inclusive options for children and parents and to maintain services for children and families across a 5-year period. We found that having administrators and other personnel in key locations within the system was essential. These individuals ensured that "administrative permission" (i.e., local policy that supported inclusion) was ongoing, provided resources (e.g., teachers, funds for the program to operate, transportation), and also provided the attention necessary for ongoing operation of the program. In the VIP program, support began at the state level, with the state early childhood special education coordinator noting, "You have to pay for the opportunity to put this child [a child with disabilities] with normally developing children," but acknowledging that "the funding formula remains problematic" (Horn et al., 1995, p. 93). At the school system level, the special education administrators discussed support for preschool inclusion as follows:

> There are some things that we're going to do because we think they're important . . . [we have] to make sure that we do not become a party to the misery that's created by underfundedness, by not appropriately focusing those resources on what we say we want to do. (Horn et al., 1995, p. 93)

This support at the administrative level allowed the early childhood coordinator in the system to work with teachers in designing a community-based program, provide training, and apply the available funding for families' access to the program and transportation for children. Our interviews and field notes from the VIP program indicated that support was sustained across the 5 years of our project, and inclusive classes became the main way of providing educational services for preschool children.

Importantly, however, support for inclusion may differ in different settings. In the VIP program, funding and administrative initiative were key supports. In the City Center Child Care (CCCC) program, the administrator's vision for a program that would include individuals (children and staff) with disabilities, and her organization of that program (i.e., planning the student makeup of the classroom, hiring staff with disabilities, providing training for new staff) to reflect her vision were essential supports. In the Vista Valley program, joint planning by the Head Start and public school administrators, providing sufficient special education staff and staff time for meaningful involvement in the classroom, and providing training when necessary were some of the supports necessary for the high quality of inclusion occurring in this program. Ongoing support across the years allowed the inclusive model to expand to other Head Start classrooms in the system.

Implications for Practice

- Proactive administrative support, in terms of a key administrator(s) advocating for the program, is essential.
- Necessary and critical support will differ across programs, but may

include adequate funding, allocation of sufficient personnel and materials, allocation of sufficient staff time to ensure that collaboration and joint planning can occur, and access to training related to inclusion.

- Ongoing support is necessary for the maintenance and growth of high-quality inclusive programs.

INCLUSION CAN BENEFIT CHILDREN WITH AND WITHOUT DISABILITIES

We did not conduct a formal study of the outcomes of preschool inclusion for children and families. Before beginning our research, we decided that we would not have enough control of programs in the community (and did not think it was a very good idea) to randomly assign children to inclusive and noninclusive programs and measure their development and learning across time. So, our insights into the benefits to children with and without disabilities were based on our observations and interviews with parents and teachers.

The larger research literature has, for years, told us that children with disabilities make at least as much developmental progress in inclusive programs as they do in noninclusive programs (Buysse & Bailey, 1993; Lamorey & Bricker, 1993; Odom & McEvoy, 1988). Furthermore, there is evidence that greater progress or more mature levels of performance may occur in communication skills, social competence, and perhaps play skills (Guralnick, Connor, Hammond, Gottman, & Kinnish, 1996; Jenkins, Odom, & Speltz, 1989). In our research, we found that in inclusive settings, children with disabilities (as a group) actively participated in the classroom as much as their classmates without disabilities, and we found that children with disabilities spent the majority of their time in small or large groups that involved peers without disabilities. About two-thirds of the children with disabilities in our research were well accepted or at least not socially rejected by their peers, although this meant, as previously noted, that about one-third of the children were socially rejected. Teachers and parents reported that most children with disabilities had at least one friendship with a peer, although the average number of friendships reported was less for children with disabilities than for typically developing peers.

Across children, parents and/or family members reported the positive effects they had seen for their children. For example, Michael's (a boy identified as having mental retardation and enrolled in the Beacon Street program) mother told us, "The test results indicated that he needed some speech encouragement . . . [Beacon Street] was the preschool place-ment recommended, an inclusive model. . . . We have seen tremendous growth in speech" (Lieber et al., 1996, p. 83). For Jimmy, the child with autism mentioned several times in this book, the teachers noted that when he began in the program (KidCorp classroom of the VIP program) he

> spent much of his time screaming and tantrumming. . . . His assistant teacher reported that several months later he could lie down on his mat at naptime, line up and stand in line with other children, allow the teacher to take him to the toilet. (Horn et al., 1995, p. 37)

Kelly, the young girl whose case description opened this book, was blind and enrolled in the Winter County classroom of the Northumberland program. Her mother told us:

> She is so independent. . . . Just a totally different child. All for the better, no, nothing for the worse I've seen at all. . . . Everybody, all my friends, family, it was like, I can't believe how much different Kelly is since she's been in school. (parent interview)

Although we saw and heard about much progress occurring for children, it is important to note that for some children the experience was not necessarily a positive one. Daniel, a boy identified as having ADHD and enrolled in the Valley View program, attended a special education class for part of the day and a Head Start program for the remainder of the day. During our observations, continuing concerns were expressed by his teacher, and also his grandmother with whom he lived, about his disruptive behavior. His Head Start teacher expressed concerns that her class had become a "dumping ground" for Daniel, and his peer group socially rejected him. Janko, Cottam, and Anderson (1997) noted in Daniel's case study, "There was not a single day during which we recorded field observations that Daniel did not have experiences that we interpreted as being punishing to him" (p. 24). In this case study, there were no reports of progress from his teachers or his grandmother. There is no question that negative outcomes sometimes occurred for some children. However, our general conclusion, across the 80 children with disabilities in our original study, was that children with disabilities were making substantial progress in inclusive settings. From the negative examples, such as Daniel's, we learned much about the barriers that exist to inclusion for individual children and what we might do to overcome those barriers.

The research literature also tells us that typically developing peers benefit from their inclusion in programs for children with disabilities

(Diamond & Innes, 2000). Benefits reported are increased knowledge of disabling conditions (Diamond, Hestenes, Carpenter, & Innes, 1997), willingness to interact with children with disabilities (Okagaki, Diamond, Kontos, & Hestenes, 1998), and more positive attitudes toward individuals with disabilities (Favazza & Odom, 1997). Again, our research did not specifically assess benefits associated with inclusion for typically developing children, but teachers and parents reported some. From our observations, we learned that typically developing peers were actively engaged in the early childhood settings and participated in groups with children with disabilities the majority of the time. Also, the typically developing children we followed were very well accepted by peers and had single and multiple friendships, as reported by teachers.

The parents of Eddie (a typically developing child enrolled in the Beacon Street program) noted as a benefit of the inclusive program, the overall educational experience their child was receiving. They pointed out that

> If they weren't teaching Eddie what he should be learning . . . and they were doing things slower for the other children, and that was holding Eddie back, now I wouldn't have liked that. But it didn't seem to be that way. (Lieber et al., 1996, p. 117)

When the teachers at the Cornwallis program were asked about the benefits for children without disabilities in their team teaching classrooms, they reported one long-term social benefit: "Inclusion provides opportunities for them [typically developing children] to understand and accept differences among people so that they will not make fun of other people" (Li, Lieber, & Beckman, 1997, p. 36). Parents from the Briar Brook program identified several benefits from the participation of their typically developing children as peer models. Steve's father said: "I think Steve will be less afraid or less likely to treat them differently or like they were strange or weird like other kids might." David's mother noted: "Definitely the tolerance that he gains to handicapped children . . . it will help him. . . . I think he is one step ahead of kids that go to a normal, everyday preschool." Jackie's, a child with disabilities, mother described a potential societal benefit: "I think that after this [inclusion] has gone on for some time, that as a society . . . people are going to be more tolerant and aware." However, it is important to note that parents occasionally expressed concern. Jeffery's, a child with ADHD, mother said, "I don't know if they realize at this age—it is almost like race—do they realize disabilities? I don't think it phases them one way or another" (all quotes from Capell et al., 1997, pp. 23–24).

Implications for Practice

- Our research was consistent with other research reviews in indicating that children with disabilities, as a group, experience developmental and social benefits from being in inclusive settings.
- Despite the overall positive benefit, inclusive experiences may not be positive for all children, so the progress and daily experiences of children with disabilities and their typically developing peers should be monitored frequently.
- Typically developing peers benefit from the overall experiences gained from early childhood settings (i.e., are not held back by the presence of children with disabilities), and their attitudes toward children with disabilities may be positively affected.

CONCLUSION

Becoming a member of the class and eventually a member of the world is an important objective for young children with disabilities. These synthesis points highlight the issues that may help children take such an important step or may place barriers in their path. Definitions and beliefs form the foundation for inclusion, which in turn influences the nature of the practices occurring in the class and the collaboration that occurs among adults. It is our hope that these will combine to help children like Kelly, Jimmy, and Kevin to all become members of the world.

REFERENCES

Billingsley, F. F., Gallucci, C., Peck, C. A., Schwartz, I. S., & Staub, D., (1996). "But those kids can't even do math": An alternative conceptualization of outcomes for inclusion education. *Special Education Leadership Review, 13*, 43–55.

Bredekamp, S., & Copple, C. (Eds.). (1997). *Developmentally appropriate practice in early childhood programs* (rev. ed.). Washington, DC: National Association for the Education of Young Children.

Bricker, D., Pretti-Fronczak, K., & McComas, N. (1998). *An activity-based approach to early intervention* (2nd ed.). Baltimore, MD: Brookes.

Buysse, V., & Bailey, D. B. (1993). Behavioral and developmental outcomes in young children with disabilities in integrated and segregated settings: A review of comparative studies. *Journal of Special Education, 26*, 434–461.

Capell, D., Greig, D., Barnwell, D., Lieber, J., Li, S., Day, M., & Beckman, P. J. (1997). *Providing models for our children: A case study of Briar Brook Inclusion Program.* Unpublished case study, University of Maryland, College Park.

Carta, J. J., Schwartz, I. S., Atwater, J. B., & McConnell, S. R. (1991). Developmentally appropriate practice: Appraising its usefulness for young children with disabilities. *Topics in Early Childhood Special Education, 11,* 1–20.

Clark, C. M., & Peterson, P. L. (1986). Teachers' thought processes. In M. Wittrock (Ed.), *Handbook of research on teaching* (3rd ed.; pp. 255–296). New York: Macmillan.

Diamond, K., Hestenes, L., Carpenter, E., & Innes, F. (1997). Relationships between enrollment in an inclusive class and preschool children's ideas about people with disabilities. *Topics in Early Childhood Special Education, 17,* 520–537.

Diamond, K. E., & Innes, F. K. (2000). The origins of young children's attitudes toward peers with disabilities. In M. Guralnick (Ed.), *Early childhood inclusion: Focus on change* (pp. 159–177). Baltimore, MD: Brookes.

Division for Early Childhood. (2000). *DEC policy statement on inclusion.* Arlington, VA: Council for Exceptional Children.

Early Childhood Research Institute on Inclusion. (1998). *Early childhood inclusion synthesis points* (ECRII Brief No. 11). Nashville, TN: Author.

Favazza, P. C., & Odom, S. L. (1997). Promoting positive attitudes of kindergarten-age children toward individuals with disabilities. *Exceptional Children, 63,* 405–422.

Guralnick, M. J., Connor, R. T., Hammond, M. A., Gottman, J. M., & Kinnish, K. (1996). Immediate effects of mainstreamed settings on the social interactions and social integration of preschool children. *American Journal on Mental Retardation, 100,* 359–377.

Hanson, M. J., Wolfberg, P., Zercher, C., Morgan, M., Gutierrez, S., Barnwell, D., & Beckman, P. J. (1998). The culture of inclusion: Recognizing diversity at multiple levels. *Early Childhood Research Quarterly, 13,* 185–209.

Hart, B., & Risley, T. (1968). Establishing use of descriptive adjectives in the spontaneous speech of disadvantaged preschool children. *Journal of Applied Behavior Analysis, 1,* 109–120.

Horn, E., Lieber, J., Sandall, S., Schwartz, I., & Shouming, L. (2000). Supporting young children's IEP goals in inclusive settings through embedded learning opportunities. *Topics in Early Childhood Special Education, 20,* 208–223.

Horn, E. M., Odom, S. L., Marquart, J. M., Pallas, P. J., & Kaiser, A. P. (1995). *Stepping out in the community: VIP case study.* Unpublished case study, Vanderbilt University, Early Childhood Research Institute on Inclusion, Nashville, TN.

Janko, S., Cottam, C., & Anderson, K. (1997). *Children like Daniel: Including children in schools and community.* Unpublished case study, University of Washington, Seattle.

Jenkins, J. R., Odom, S. L., & Speltz, M. L. (1989). Effects of integration and structured play on the development of handicapped children. *Exceptional Children, 55,* 420–428.

Kaiser, A. P., & Hester, P. (1994). Generalized effects of enhanced milieu training. *Journal of Speech and Hearing Research, 17,* 1320–1340.

Koegel, L. K., Koegel, R. L., Harrower, J. K., & Carter, C. M. (1999). Pivotal response intervention I: Overview of approach. *Journal of the Association for Persons with Severe Disabilities, 24,* 174–185.

Lamorey, S., & Bricker, D. D. (1993). Integrated programs: Effects on young children and their parents. In C. Peck, S. Odom, & D. Bricker (Eds.), *Integrating young children with disabilities into community-based programs: Ecological perspectives on research and implementation* (pp. 249–269). Baltimore, MD: Brookes.

Li, S., Lieber, J., & Beckman, P. J. (1997). *In search of a common vision: A case study of Cornwallis Elementary School.* Unpublished case study, University of Maryland, College Park.

Lieber, J., Beckman, P. J., Hanson, M. J., Janko, S., Marquart, J. M., Horn, E., & Odom, S. L. (1997). The impact of changing roles on relationships between professionals in inclusive programs for young children. *Early Education and Development, 8,* 67–82.

Lieber, J., Beckman, P., Li, S., Herring, K., & Barnwell, D. (1996). *Implementing inclusion by minimizing the differences: A case study of Beacon Street Elementary School.* Unpublished case study, University of Maryland, College Park.

Lieber, J., Capell, K., Sandall, S. R., Wolfberg, P., Horn, E., & Beckman, P. J. (1998). Inclusive preschool programs: Teachers' beliefs and practices. *Early Childhood Research Quarterly, 13,* 87–105.

Marquart, J. M., & Tabor, S. (1998). *Out of boxes and into the mainstream: A case study of system-wide preschool inclusion.* Unpublished case study, Vanderbilt University, Nashville, TN.

Odom, S. L., Horn, E. M., Marquart, J., Hanson, M. J., Wolfberg, P., Beckman, P. J., Lieber, J., Li, S., Schwartz, I., Janko, S., & Sandall, S. (1999). On the forms of inclusion: Organizational context and individualized service delivery models. *Journal of Early Intervention, 22,* 185–199.

Odom, S. L., & McEvoy, M. A. (1988). Integration of young children with handicaps and normally developing children. In S. Odom & M. Karnes (Eds.), *Early intervention for infants and children with handicaps: An empirical base* (pp. 241–268). Baltimore, MD: Brookes.

Okagaki, L., Diamond, K. E., Kontos, S. J., & Hestenes, L. L. (1998). Correlates of young children's interactions with classmates with disabilities. *Early Childhood Research Quarterly, 13,* 67–86.

Rule, S., Losardo, A., Dinnebeil, L., Kaiser, A., & Rowland, C. (1998). Translating research on naturalistic instruction into practice. *Journal of Early Intervention, 21,* 283–293.

Sandall, S. R., Joseph, G., Chou, H., Schwartz, I. S., Horn, E., Lieber, J., Odom, S. L., & Wolery, R. (in press). Talking to practitioners: Focus group report on curriculum modifications in inclusive preschool classrooms. *Journal of Early Intervention.*

Sandall, S., McLean, M. E., & Smith, B. J. (2000). *DEC recommended practices in early intervention/early childhood special education.* Longmont, CO: Sopris West.

Schwartz, I. S., Odom, S. L., & Sandall, S. R. (1999). Including young children with special needs. *Child Care Information Exchange, 130,* 74–78.

U.S. Department of Education. (1999). *To assure the free appropriate public education of all children with disabilities: Twenty-first annual report to Congress on the implementation of the Individuals with Disabilities Education Act*. Washington, DC: Author.

Wolery, M., Strain, P. S., & Bailey, D. B. (1992). Reaching potentials for children with special needs. In S. Bredekamp & T. Rosegrant (Eds.), *Reaching potentials: Appropriate curriculum and assessment for young children* (Vol. 1, pp. 92–112). Washington, DC: National Association for the Education of Young Children.

Wolery, R. A., & Odom, S. L. (2000). *An administrator's guide to preschool inclusion*. Chapel Hill, NC: Frank Porter Graham Child Development Center.

Wolfberg, P., Hanson, M. J., & Zercher, C. (1995). *Santa Luna Head Start case study*. Unpublished case study, San Francisco State University, San Francisco.

The Ecological Systems Study

THE FIRST STUDY OF OUR PROJECT was called the ecological systems study. Our goal in this study was to describe the social ecology in which children with disabilities and typically developing children in their preschool classes were embedded. Through this description, we hoped to learn about the barriers to and facilitators of preschool inclusion.

SETTINGS

Our original team of researchers were located in four regions in the United States: the mid-South, the mid-eastern seaboard, the Pacific Northwest, and the San Francisco Bay Area of California. At each location, we asked administrators of special education and Head Start programs to help us find classes in which children with disabilities participated with typically developing children. We were interested in finding programs that used different approaches to inclusion, operated in different settings, provided services to children and families from different cultural and socioeconomic groups, and were located in urban, suburban, and rural areas. As mentioned in Chapter 1, we used a broad definition of inclusion (i.e., children with and without disabilities in the some classrooms) and let administrators define the inclusive programs.

Sixteen programs, four from each region, participated in the study. The features of these programs are described in Table A.1. It is important to understand that some programs operated in different classroom settings (Santa Luna, VIP), while some programs operated in a single or small number of classrooms (Beacon Street, Briar Brook). A short description of each program appears in Appendix B.

In our later analysis of these programs, we found that each could be described by two general characteristics: organizational contexts and individualized-service models. Organizational context is the "primary administrative or programmatic agency or agencies in which the inclusive classrooms exist" (Odom et al., 1999, p. 188). Inclusive programs were

Table A.1. Program Characteristics

Site	Name	Location	Family SES	Ethnicity of Children	Number of Classes	Children Without Disabilities per Class (mean n)	Children with Disabilities per Class (mean n)	Adults per Class (mean n)
1	Santa Luna	Urban/suburban	Low	Latino, White, Asian/Pacific Islander, Black, Arab, African, East Indian, Multiracial	5	17.2	3	2
1	Hathaway	Urban	Low-middle	Black, Latino, White, Asian/Pacific Islander, Arab, Multiracial	3	22.5	2.6	5.5
1	Vista Valley	Rural	Low-middle	Latino, White, Black, Multiracial	2	15	3	5
1	Costa Mesa	Urban	Low-middle	Asian/Pacific Islander, White, Black, Latino, Multiracial	2	26	13	8
2	Winwood	Urban	Low	Black, White, Multiracial	2	17	8	2
2	Beacon Street	Urban	Low-middle	Black, White	1	17	7	4
2	Briar Brook	Suburban	Middle	White	1	2	7	2
2	Cornwallis	Urban	Low	Black	1	19	7	4
3	VIP	Urban/suburban	Low-middle	White, Black, Multiracial	5	2	1.2	3.4
3	Rolling Hills	Rural	Low	White, Black	2	14.5	5	2
3	Lincoln County	Urban/suburban	Low-middle	White, Black, Latino, Asian, Multiracial	2	20	5	4
3	Northumberland	Rural/Suburban	Low-middle	White, Black, Multiracial	2	10.5	9.5	4
4	Building Blocks	Urban	Low	Asian/Pacific Islander, Black, Latino, White, Multiracial	2	14	2	2
4	City Center	Urban	Low-middle	White, Black, Asian/Pacific Islander, Latino, Multiracial	4	11.3	2.75	3.25
4	Hidden Trails	Suburban	Low-middle	White, Black, Latino	2	13	3.5	2
4	Valley View	Rural	Middle	White, Asian	1	16	16	3

Notes. See Appendix B for site descriptions. Reprinted with permission from " On the Forms of Inclusion: Organizational Context and Service Delivery Models," by S. L. Odom et al., 1999, *Journal of Early Intervention, 22,* 185–199.

located in community-based child care centers, Head Start programs, and public school early childhood education programs. We describe each of these program types in Figure A.1a and discuss the social policy issues that existed for each organizational context in Chapter 9.

Individualized service models describe the ways in which instructional or therapy programs were delivered to children with disabilities. These models are itinerant teaching–direct service, itinerant teaching–collaborative/consultative, team teaching, early childhood education, early childhood special education, and integrative activities. Descriptions of each of these models appear in Figure A.1b. In Chapters 3 and 6 we

---

Community-Based Child Care: Children are enrolled in child care or preschool programs operated outside the public school system. The program may be publicly or privately located or funded, but not affiliated with or funded by Head Start.

Head Start: Children are enrolled in programs administered by Head Start; these may be located separate from or within public school buildings. The key feature is that the Head Start agency administers the funds and oversees the program.

Public School Early Childhood Education: Children are enrolled in early childhood education or early childhood special education classes operating through the public school, but are not Head Start classes. Funding sources may include (singly or in combination) Chapter 1, state, local, corporate, or private funds.

Public School–Head Start Combination: Children are enrolled in Head Start classrooms for which the public school system is the contracting agency. Classrooms may or may not be located in public school buildings. Funding may come from sources in addition to Head Start.

Public School–Child Care: Children are enrolled in child care programs managed by the public school system in which families pay tuition.

Dual Enrollment: Children are enrolled in an early childhood education program for part of the day and other types of specialized programs (inclusive or nonintegrated special education) for other parts of the day.

Figure A.1a. Definitions of organizational contexts. *Note.* Figures A.1a and A.1b are reprinted with permission from "On the Forms of Inclusion: Organizational Context and Individualized Service Delivery Models," by S. L. Odom et al., 1999, *Journal of Early Intervention, 22,* 185–199.

Itinerant Teaching–Direct Service: Services are provided on a regular basis in early childhood education settings by special education teachers and related service personnel. Itinerant teachers or other related service personnel visit the settings rather than being housed there permanently. Educational or therapy goals for individual children are not systematically embedded in the curriculum activities or classroom routines by these specialists.

Itinerant Teaching–Collaborative/Consultative: Special education teachers and related service personnel work with the early childhood teacher to systematically embed individualized educational goals for children in curriculum activities and classroom routines.

Team Teaching: An early childhood teacher and a special education teacher both occupy teacher roles in the same classroom. They may collaborate in planning, jointly implement educational activities, and share classroom space. Related services are provided in the classroom.

Early Childhood Education: An early childhood teacher assumes the primary responsibility for planning, implementing, and monitoring classroom activities for children with and without disabilities, with little contact with other special education or related service personnel.

Early Childhood Special Education: A special education teacher assumes primary responsibility for planning, implementing, and monitoring classroom activities, with little contact or collaboration with an early childhood education teacher. Children without disabilities are brought into the classroom.

Integrative Activities: Children with disabilities and children without disabilities spend a majority of the day in separate classes but participate in joint activities for a portion of the day, then return to their respective classrooms. The majority of special education and related services are provided in the separate classroom.

Figure A.1b. Definitions of individualized-service models.

discuss issues related to instructional approaches and collaboration for these models.

PARTICIPANTS

In each inclusive program, we asked teachers to help select five children with disabilities to participate in our study. Children with disabilities had to meet the state's requirements for receiving special education services and had to have an IEP. At least two of the five children had to have a severe developmental delay, behavior disorder, or multiple disabilities. We also asked teachers to help us include children from different socioeconomic and cultural groups as well as a good mix of boys and girls. In addition to the five children with disabilities, two typically developing children from each program also participated. The typically developing children were selected based on their similarity to one of the children with disabilities from their classroom who was involved in the study (i.e., gender, chronological age, ethnic background, socioeconomic level). We obtained consent from the parents for their children's and their own participation in the study; we also obtained consent from teachers and administrators.

In all, 112 children (80 children with disabilities and 32 typically developing children) and their families participated in this study. Descriptions of the children and their families appear in Tables A.2a–A.2c. Children in this study had a range of disabilities, came from different ethnic groups, and were spread across the preschool age range. Also, parents had different marital status, education levels, and employment status. We felt that we had a group of children and parents in our study that represented fairly well the demographics of children with disabilities in this country.

METHODS

To gain a comprehensive understanding of how inclusion worked in these 16 inclusive preschool programs, we gathered a range of quantitative and qualitative information (see Figure A.2). At the beginning of our study, we assessed each child using the Battelle Developmental Inventory in order to describe children's development in a consistent way. We also observed the children in regular class activities using a system called the Code for the Active Student Participation and Engagement—Revised (CASPER) (Brown, Odom, & Favazza, 1995). Children were observed six times for 30 minutes each. The CASPER provided information about the ecological features of the classroom (with whom the child participated in activities, the types of activities, whether the teacher or child initiated the activities) and children's and adults' behavior. We describe the CASPER in more detail in Chapter 3. After each CASPER observation, we also gathered information (using an observer impressions scale) on the children's social interactions with peers as well as examples of "stand-out" (participating appropriately in class) and "stick-out" (not behaving like a member of the class). All children in the class completed a peer-rating

Table A.2a. Demographic Characteristics—Children

	%	*n*
Age		
3 years	26.8	30
4 years	56.2	63
5 years	17.0	19
Gender		
Male	58.0	65
Female	42.0	47
Race or ethnicity		
White/Caucasian	54.5	61
Black/African American	24.1	27
Latino/Hispanic (of any race)	8.0	9
Asian/Pacific Islander	8.0	9
Native American	.9	1
Multiracial	4.5	5
Disability		
Speech/language impairment	17.8	20
Developmental delay	11.6	13
Mental retardation	10.7	12
Physical impairment	9.8	11
Autism/pervasive developmental delay	8.9	10
Social-emotional, behavioral, or attention deficit disorder	5.4	6
Hearing impairment	1.8	2
Visual impairment	2.7	3
Health impairment	2.7	3
None	28.6	32
Age at identification of disability		
Birth to 1 year	22.3	25
1-2 years	7.1	8
2-3 years	22.3	25
3-4 years	14.3	16
4-5 years	1.8	2
Not applicable/not reported	32.2	36
	($N = 112$)	

Note. Tables A.2a–A.2c reprinted with permission from "On the Forms of Inclusion: Organizational Context and Individualized Service Delivery Models," by S. L. Odom et al., 1999, *Journal of Early Intervention, 22,* 185–199.

Table A.2b. Demographic Characteristics—Caregivers

	Mother in Household (n = 99)		Father in Household (n = 64)	
	%	n	%	n
Marital status				
Single	26.3	26	1.6	1
Married/partnered	62.6	62	93.7	60
Divorced/separated/widowed	11.1	11	4.7	3
Educational level				
Less than high school	16.2	16	12.5	8
High school graduate	29.3	29	21.9	14
Vocational training	3.0	3	3.1	2
Some college	15.2	15	18.8	12
Associate degree	5.0	5	3.1	2
College degree	18.2	18	28.1	18
Advanced degree	9.1	9	12.5	8
Not reported	4.0	4	0.0	0
Employment status				
Not employed	37.4	37	12.5	8
Part-time employed	24.2	24	12.5	8
Full-time employed	35.4	35	73.4	47
Not reported	3.0	3	1.6	1

Notes. Based on 112 households. In 11 households, caregivers were grandparents, other relatives, or foster parents, or were not reported.

assessment, in which they told us whom they liked to play with "a lot," "a little," or "not at all" (Asher, Singleton, Tinsley, & Hymel, 1979). Also, we asked teachers and parents to tell us about the child's reciprocal friendships (Buysse, 1993). Last, we asked teachers to complete a survey that told us how they modified their classroom and/or curriculum for children with disabilities.

The qualitative measures were also an important source of information. Some of us, not involved in the CASPER data collection, also observed in classroom settings and wrote in our field notes about the types of activities occurring, the adult interactions, and the children's interac-

Table A.2c.   Demographic Characteristics—Households

	%	n
Income		
$15,000 or below	33.9	38
$15,001 to 30,000	15.2	17
$30,001 to 45,000	12.5	14
$45,001 to 60,000	16.1	18
Over $60,000	13.4	15
Not reported	8.9	10
Additional benefits received[a]		
None	46.4	52
Medicaid	28.6	32
AFDC	20.5	23
Supplemental Security Income (SSI)	18.8	21
WIC	12.5	14
Food stamps	12.5	14
Public housing	6.3	7
Other	4.5	5
Not reported	8.0	9

Note. Based on 112 households.
[a] Multiple responses possible.

tions. We usually observed for 3–4 hours a day, 2–3 days per week, from 1–3 months. We also conducted extensive interviews with parents, all professional and paraprofessional staff involved in providing services to children, and administrators at centers and/or school systems. These interviews were audiotaped and transcribed. The length of the parent interviews varied from one hour on a single day to several hours over several days. Also, for some of our parents, we conducted interviews again in the third and fifth years of our research. The interviews with teachers, other professionals and paraprofessionals, and administrators/ policy makers usually lasted between 1 and 2 hours. We followed a semistructured format, with protocols, that focused our conversations on several key questions related to inclusion, barriers, and facilitators. This format allowed the individuals being interviewed to take the lead in the conversation, and our interviewers to offer "probe questions" if the conversations went astray. Last, we collected documents that described

---

QUANTITATIVE INFORMATION

- Battelle Developmental Inventory
- CASPER observations
- Post-CASPER Observer Impression Scale
- Peer-rating assessment
- Friendship questionnaire for parents and teachers
- Curriculum modification survey

QUALITATIVE INFORMATION

- Nonparticipant/participant observation and field notes
- Interviews with parents
- Interviews with teachers, assistants, and related service staff
- Interviews with program directors, special education supervisors, and other administrators related to the program
- Interviews with state or agency level administrators

Figure A. 2. Quantitative and qualitative information collected in the ecological systems study.

the program. These documents include program brochures, newspaper articles, operational or procedural handbooks, and so forth.

DATA ANALYSIS

With the great amount of data collected, data analysis became a paramount concern. We could easily summarize the quantitative data and share them with our research colleagues across sites. However, the qualitative data were not as easily managed. In order to reduce the data to a manageable form, we began by creating case studies for each of our programs. At each site, we selected one program that would serve as an intensive case study. At the end of the first year of our research, we met in California to share these intensive case studies and begin identifying themes that appeared to be emerging from the data. Dr. David Fetterman, our methodological consultant, led this data-analysis meeting. The initial themes we identified then guided us in our further data collection at the other sites and construction of the subsequent case studies. Ongoing data sharing and data analysis occurred through frequent conference calls and e-mail correspondence. During the second year, we again met as a group, with Dr. Fetterman as the leader, shared case studies, and refined the themes that had become a part of our analysis. The pattern of biweekly (or more frequent) conference calls, weekly and sometimes daily e-mail correspondence, and face-to-face meetings, usually at least twice a year to share and analyze data, continued for the entire 5-year project.

When themes were identified, one or two investigators served as leaders of a study team. The team began by focusing the question or questions they were going to address and then looking for data sources that would provide information about the theme. For example, for the theme of social relationships, all investigators used the case studies or summaries to understand the contexts of each site, but the detailed analysis of the theme required that we go back to our CASPER observations, peer-rating assessment, friendship questionnaire, field note observations, and interviews to uncover information about social acceptance and social rejection of children. For other themes (parent perspectives), we depended on one or two sources of data (parent interviews), although these data came from the four sites. We routinely followed the constant comparative method (Glaser & Strauss, 1967) when our data source was qualitative in nature (e.g., field note observations). When our data analysis involved mixed methods, we often followed a data-analysis technique that sought complementary support for the conclusions we drew from the data (Li, Marquart, & Zercher, 2000). Our individual research studies describe in detail the specific methodology we followed.

INDIVIDUAL RESEARCH STUDIES

The ecological systems study was the foundation for our later research. In the third and fifth years of our project, we returned to each of the programs in the ecological systems study to see if they had changed across time and to learn about influences that may have led to the changes (see Chapter 9).

In addition to the ecological systems study and our study of program maintenance, we also conducted individual research studies on curriculum modifications, specific teaching strategies, family perspectives, collaboration, community participation, social policy, and costs/finance. In these studies we used a range of experimental research methodologies and information sources, such as single-subject design, focus-group discussion, large-scale surveys, semistructured interviews, field note observations, and cost analyses. In Chapters 3–10 we provide references to the studies that produced the findings we describe, and we refer the reader to the specific studies cited for descriptions of the methodology.

REFERENCES

Asher, S. R., Singleton, L. C., Tinsley, B. R., & Hymel, S. (1979). A reliable sociometric measure for preschool children. *Developmental Psychology, 15,* 443–444.

Brown, W. H., Odom, S. L., & Favazza, P. C. (1995). *Code for the active student participation and engagement—revised (CASPER II): A training manual for observers.* Vanderbilt University, Nashville, TN.

Buysse, V. (1993). Friendships of preschoolers with disabilities in community-based child care settings. *Journal of Early Intervention, 17,* 380–395.

Glaser, B., & Strauss, A. L. (1967). *The discovery of grounded theory: Strategies for qualitative research.* Chicago: Aldine.

Li, S., Marquart, J. M., & Zercher, C. (2000). Conceptual issues and analytic strategies in mixed-method studies of preschool inclusion. *Journal of Early Intervention, 23,* 116–132.

Odom, S. L., Horn, E. M., Marquart, J., Hanson, M. J., Wolfberg, P., Beckman, P. J., Lieber, J., Li, S., Schwartz, I., Janko, S., & Sandall, S. (1999). On the forms of inclusion: Organizational context and individualized service delivery models. *Journal of Early Intervention, 22,* 185–199.

APPENDIX B

Program Descriptions

SITE 1

Program 1: Santa Luna County Head Start

Santa Luna County Head Start is located in an urban/suburban community in northern California. The system runs 36 preschool classrooms in 10 different centers throughout the county. The program serves approximately 568 low-income families and their children ages 3 to 5 years. The families represent diverse ethnic and cultural groups, including a large Latino population. At the time of our study, a total of 85 children with disabilities were enrolled in the program and fully included within preschool classes.

We conducted research in five of these classrooms. In the classrooms there were an average of 3 children with IEPs, out of an average total class enrollment of 17.2. Two of the children had dual enrollment in Head Start and a special day class in the public schools. The classes were semi-bilingual, taught in English and Spanish. An early childhood teacher model was used to deliver special education services. The Head Start teachers were the lead teachers in the classroom. Consultants occasionally provided IEP-related services on site. Parents were primarily responsible for accessing school district special education support services.

Program 2: Hathaway Preschool

Hathaway Preschool is located in a small urban community within a heavily populated area of northern California. At this site, two existing programs operating within the public schools work together to provide an inclusion option. One early childhood education program is state and federally funded for typically developing children whose parents meet income criteria, work and/or go to school, and need child care. The second is an early childhood special education program funded by the public schools. The programs run three preschool classes and one special day

187

class serving approximately 72 children ages 3 to 5 years. The children represent diverse ethnic and cultural groups, which include a large African American population. At the time of our study, 12 children with disabilities were enrolled in the program, with about half fully included.

We conducted research in the preschool classes that included children with disabilities for half-day sessions, 4 out of 5 days a week. There were 2–3 children with IEPs added to a class enrollment of 20–30 children. Special education services were provided through an itinerant teaching model that combined both direct services and collaborative/consultative approaches. Early childhood teachers were the head teachers, while a special education teacher rotated among classrooms. Both early childhood and special education assistants worked within classrooms. The children received related special education services on a pull-out basis within the school site.

Program 3: Vista Valley Head Start

Vista Valley Head Start is located in a relatively small rural community in northern California. At this site, the Head Start program and local school district have combined to provide inclusive programs for children. The Head Start program runs nine preschool centers and two home-based programs serving more than 270 low-income families and their children ages 3 to 5 years. The families reflect diverse ethnic and cultural groups, with the majority Latino. Over 10% of the children served have disabilities. The program offers mainstreaming, integration, and full inclusion options.

We conducted research in the one center providing full inclusion in two preschool classrooms. Each classroom consisted of a class enrollment of 18 children, three of whom had IEPs. The classes were bilingual, taught in Spanish and English. Special education services were carried out through an itinerant collaborative/consultative teaching model. The Head Start teacher was the lead teacher, while a special education teacher functioned as a support teacher across classrooms. Both Head Start and special education assistants worked within classrooms. All support services were coordinated between the special education program and Head Start. The children received some related services in class and others on a pull-out basis on site.

Program 4: Costa Mesa Children's Center

Costa Mesa Children's Center is located in a large urban community in northern California. At this site, a special education program is co-located with a child development center run by the school district. The program runs nine preschool classes and an after-school program that includes children ages 3 to 8 years. The child development center receives state and federal funding and serves more than 200 children whose families meet income criteria, work and/or go to school, and need child care. The special education program is funded by the public schools and serves 33 children with disabilities in three special day classes. The majority of children with disabilities are White, while those without disabilities are Asian.

We conducted our research in a special day class consisting of 13 children with disabilities and an early childhood education class with 26 typically developing children. A flexible wall separated the two classrooms. For a portion of the day, the teachers opened up the divider for the two groups to combine for integrated/inclusive activities. The groups also participated jointly in other activities during the day, such as lunch, outdoor play, and weekly field trips. The children received all related services on a pull-out basis on site.

SITE 2

Program 1: Winwood Special Center

Located in one of the largest school systems in the nation, Winwood is one of four early childhood centers that serve children with disabilities from birth through age 8. It is unique among the early childhood centers in its county in that it also serves typically developing 4-year-old children that qualify for Head Start or for the state-funded prekindergarten program. There are a relatively small number of Head Start classes, six, at this center; most of the typically developing 4-year-olds are served in the state-funded program. The Head Start programs are funded 60% by the school district and 40% by the federal government. There are 500 children with disabilities at this center and 200 children without disabilities. The school is situated in a nonresidential, industrial area. It serves a primarily poor and lower-middle-income area that is a suburb of a large eastern city.

In this program, which at the time of our study had been in existence for 4 years, a class of children with disabilities and the children from the Head Start class across the hall participate in a joint activity for 30 minutes a day. During the remainder of the day the children are in separate classrooms. In the joint activity both classes may merge completely, or the Head Start teacher may lead an activity with half Head Start/half special education students in her room, while the special education teacher leads an activity with a similar mix of children in her room. Thus, this program uses an integrative-activities approach. Special education services are provided to the children by the special education teacher and related service personnel in the special education classroom or on a pull-out basis. In the special education class there are 8 children; the Head Start class has 17 children. Both teachers are certified in special education. The Head Start teacher also has certification in early childhood. Ninety-five percent of the children in both classes are African American.

Program 2: Beacon Street

This is an inner-city public school program in a large urban system. It serves a combination of poor urban neighborhoods as well as a middle-income neighborhood that is becoming gentrified. The system has 179 schools, including 119 elementary, 28 middle, 14 high, 10 special education, 5 alternative, and 3 vocational/technical schools. Most preschool children with disabilities are served in self-contained classrooms; however, there are six programs, including this one, within the local education agency that combine a class for children with disabilities with a prekindergarten class using a co-teaching approach.

This program, which at the time of our study was in its fourth year, is the model on which the other five programs in the city are based. It is located in an elementary school in a working-class neighborhood that is experiencing gentrification. Each half-day session has 17 children with disabilities and 7 children without disabilities. The school improvement team has elected to continue its prekindergarten program even though the school is no longer classified as a Chapter 1 school. The prekindergarten class is funded using the school budget. Therefore, there are no income requirements for the children who are enrolled; neighborhood children are offered the program on a first-come, first-served basis. The children with disabilities come from the neighborhood as well as from surrounding areas, since there is not a preschool special education program in each elementary school. The class is co-taught by a special education teacher and an early education teacher. Related services, including speech and occupational therapy, are provided within the blended classroom. Half the class is African American and half European American.

Program 3: Briar Brook

This program is located in an elementary school in a relatively small middle- to upper-middle-income suburban county. The program is one of eight Regional Early Childhood Centers (RECCs) that serve children from birth through kindergarten age with disabilities in the district. In this RECC program, there are several teachers who work with infants and toddlers, three preschool programs, and an inclusive kindergarten classroom.

The district has chosen to implement a reverse mainstreaming approach at the preschool level. This classroom has seven children with disabilities and two children without disabilities who attended the half-day session that we observed. Typically developing children are recruited through the elementary school newsletter, screened (using the DIAL-R), and selected to be in one of the three preschool programs at the school. Parents of the typically developing children are charged $75 a month for the program and must provide their own transportation. Typically developing children are sought for the program to serve as models (of appropriate language and social behavior) and as "helpers" for the children with disabilities. A special education teacher leads the class and has an assistant teacher. The assistant, in this classroom, happens to have a degree in elementary education. Related services (including speech, occupational therapy, vision services, and an interpreter) are provided for the children within ongoing classroom activities. Children in this classroom are primarily White and come from middle-class families.

Program 4: Cornwallis Elementary

The context for this program is the same as for Program 2. It is also housed in an elementary school in a large urban area. When we studied the program, the classrooms contained 19 typically developing children and 7 children with disabilities in half-day sessions. A special education teacher and an early education teacher co-teach the class. Related services (speech) are provided to children within the classroom routine, as well as on a pull-out basis. Each teacher has a bachelor's degree. The children in the program are all African American and are from low-income families. Children are typically from neighborhoods in which there is relatively high crime and drugs.

SITE 3

Program 1: VIP

VIP is the preschool special education program for a local education agency (LEA) located in a moderate-sized city in the southeastern region of the United States. The population of this city is around 750,000, with a metropolitan area of nearly a million people. The public school system provides services for about 70,000 children, with approximately 10,000 qualifying for special education services. Preschool children with disabilities represent 3% of the population of children with disabilities. A full continuum of individual service models is provided for preschool children, from speech therapy services only to full-day multidisciplinary services. Two primary models are used to serve children who have needs across developmental areas that require input from educators and other related services: (1) regular school-based preschool special education classes and (2) community-based preschool and child care sites in which special education services are provided on site.

The focus of our case study was the inclusive preschool model. The model has the following components: (1) participation in a community preschool or child care center with same-aged peers for the educational portion of the day, with the tuition or fee paid by the LEA; (2) regular visits by a visiting (itinerant) preschool special educator to support the child's placement, and implementation and monitoring of the IEP; (3) provision of related services to the child in the community setting; and (4) transportation to and from the program provided at no cost to the family. Typically, only one child with a disability is enrolled in a classroom. The system strives to maintain a natural portion of children with and without disabilities. A wide range of community programs is used, including Head Start, subsidized child care programs, employer-supported programs, national child care chains, and private church-based preschool enrichment centers. We conducted research on children in five different child care/preschool centers. Program communities included the full range of diversity found in the city, from lower to upper income, blue collar/white collar, White and African American, and various religious affiliations (e.g., none, Unitarian, Methodist, Baptist, Jewish, Mormon).

Program 2: Rolling Hills Head Start

This is a small Head Start program operated under the auspices of a community action agency and located in three rural counties in middle Tennessee. The program operates in nine different centers and serves 192 children. Of those 192 children, 38 have an identified disability and an IEP. Half of the centers in this program are located in a public school building in the community, while the others are in stand-alone locations such as a portable building. An early childhood education model is implemented in which the Head Start teachers have primary responsibility for implementing the children's educational goals. The Head Start programs located in the public school have transportation and meals provided through the school system, and have some access to the special service personnel in the school. The stand-alone classrooms have a combined cook/bus driver and limited or no access to support service personnel. Some related services may be provided on an itinerant basis to both types of centers.

We conducted research in two centers in different counties. Buttermilk Station is a small town (1,000–2,000 people) located in a rural farming area. It was settled by Irish Catholic immigrants who were brought in to build the railroad through this area in the mid-nineteenth century. The two schools in the town are a consolidated K–12 public school and a Catholic elementary school that has been in existence for over 130 years. The community is predominantly White. Buttermilk Station Head Start is located in the consolidated K–12 school. Five children in the classroom have IEPs. Four of them receive speech therapy at the school, while physical therapy is provided to one child by an itinerant therapist. Another child receives services once a week from the special education teacher in a resource room in the school. The River Bend center is located in a portable building on the old school grounds in the town. River Bend is a small town that is located off the interstate. The center opened in this location the year before our study began. Five children in the classroom have IEPs. They receive no special services.

Program 3: Lincoln County Public Schools

Lincoln County Public Schools, with an enrollment of 93,000 students, is one of the twelve largest school systems in the country. It is located in a metropolitan area of nearly a million people in the upper southeast. Nearly 13,000 students in the school system received special education services during the 1995–96 school year, including almost 1,000 three- to five-year-olds. Virtually all (97%) preschool-aged children with disabilities are placed in inclusive classrooms in public schools or in private preschools/child care centers in the community. A philosophy of inclusive preschool placement has been in operation since 1988, and the public preschool options have grown each year due to the creative use of funding sources (Chapter 1, Head Start, state, corporate, and private, among others) and the expansion of preschool options. The types of public preschool classrooms include state-funded prekindergarten, tuition-based, Head Start (contract with the school system), and Jump Start (a program for at-risk 3-year-olds). The community-based option provides placements in public and private preschools and child care centers. This program model has these components: (1) placement in a public school or communnity-based early childhood classroom, with the educational portion of the day paid for by the school system; (2) regular visits by an itinerant ECSE teacher to support the child's placement, and implementation and monitoring of the IEP; (3) provision of related services to the child at the school or community setting; and (4) system-wide transportation. A collaborative service model is implemented that includes coordination among the ECSE teacher, classroom teacher, and related service personnel.

We conducted research in one combined Head Start and pre-K classroom (blended federal and state funds) and one tuition-based classroom. The combined class is located in a suburban school building that has five preschool classrooms and other, adult education programs. All children are bused to this school. In the classroom of 20 children, there were three children with disabilities. This ethnically diverse class included African American, Latino, White, and biracial children. The adult staff were a Head Start teacher and assistant teacher, and a special education assistant. The tuition-based classroom is located in a large suburban elementary school in a middle- to upper-middle-income neighborhood. Parents provide transportation for their children. This classroom of 20 children included seven children with delays/disabilities. One child was Asian American, and the others were White. There was a lead teacher, assistant teacher, and two special education assistants.

Program 4: Northumberland Head Start

The Northumberland Head Start agency operates 29 classrooms in 19 centers in eight counties. The agency serves approximately 580 four-year-old children in the centers, with another 100 three-year-old children in home-based services. The eight counties circle a moderate-sized city and thus represent both rural and suburban areas. The agency has adopted the Creative Curriculum for all its classroom-based services. Children with disabilities have been provided primarily speech therapy services in addition to the typical program. However, in the 2 years preceding our study, the agency developed two classrooms in which children with identified disabilities are included. These classrooms are cooperative agreements with the local LEA; each class has an ECSE teacher and assistant paid for by the school system and a Head Start lead and assistant teacher paid for by Northumberland. These two classrooms were the focus of our case study.

The Mayberry Head Start program is located in the community center of the small town of Mayberry (approximately 7,000 people). Mayberry is the county seat for a rural farming county (population 10,000). There are only two other incorporated towns in this county, and the school system is a county-wide program with three "grammar" schools and one high school. The focus classroom was set up as a team teaching situation with five children with disabilities (including diagnoses of physical impairments, serious health impairment, developmental delay, Down syndrome, and pervasive development delay) and 15 typically developing Head Start children. Children were provided related services, including speech, occupational, and physical therapies, as determined appropriate by the IEP team. The Winter County Head Start program is located in a suburban county adjacent to the larger city. The community has a mix of low- to middle-income families, many of whom commute to the larger city for work. The focus classroom has a team teaching model with an average of 9.5 children with disabilities and 10.5 children without disabilities. Children are primarily White, with 20–30 African American.

SITE 4

Program 1: Building Blocks

Building Blocks is an inner-city program that provides a variety of child and family services. One of the services is a Head Start program for preschoolers. There are four half-day classes. Typically, there are 2–3 children with disabilities in a class of 15 children. The program is ethnically diverse. Many families and staff are first-generation Americans. Families in Head Start meet the income criteria, and families of children with disabilities are, for the most part, below the federal poverty level. Children with disabilities are in classrooms in which the Head Start teacher is the lead teacher. For some of the children, this is their primary educational placement. The school district provides additional services through an itinerant teacher or therapist who provides direct service to children on a regular weekly schedule. Other children attend nonintegrated special education classrooms for part of the day and the Head Start classroom for the other part of the day. The Head Start teacher may provide input for the development of the IEP, but implementation is the responsibility of the itinerant teacher or therapist.

Program 2: Hidden Trails Public Schools

This is a large suburban school district. Preschool-aged children with disabilities are placed in segregated developmental preschool classrooms, community-based preschool classrooms located in elementary schools, or

Head Start classrooms. In the community-based classrooms there are five children with disabilities in a class of 16. In the Head Start classrooms, there are typically 1–2 children with disabilities in a class of 17 children. Families are predominately White and middle class. However, there is some ethnic and economic diversity.

In the Head Start classroom, the Head Start teacher is the lead teacher. An itinerant special education teacher provides direct services to children with IEPs within the classroom on a regular weekly schedule. The itinerant teacher develops and implements the IEP; the Head Start teacher is not involved in the process. In the community-based program, the children with disabilities receive services from therapists directly in the classroom. The classroom teacher is a general education teacher with special education endorsement. The classroom teacher develops and implements the IEP with assistance from families and related service professionals.

Program 3: City Center Child Care

This is a nonprofit child care center that provides child care and education services for children 4 months through 5 years of age, with and without disabilities. The center is located in a residential, densely populated urban area. The majority of families live within several miles of the center. Families are predominately White and middle class. There is some diversity in income and ethnicity. Approximately 25% of families are non-White/European American. Approximately 70% of families pay 100% of their child's tuition. Children with disabilities receive funding from other sources such as state and federal funds. The center also maintains two child care slots for families who are homeless and several slots for therapeutic care.

The child care and development program at City Center is part of a larger, long-established and financially secure nonprofit organization that serves persons with disabilities throughout their life span. Of the approximately 32 center employees, nine have disabilities. Children are grouped in multiaged, family-style arrangements. In classes for children aged 4 months through 3 years, there were usually 10 children, 3–4 of whom were children with disabilities. Children with disabilities in these classrooms receive services from therapists and other specialists within their classrooms. In classes for children aged 3 through 5 years, there were approximately 17 children, 3–4 of whom had disabilities. Children with disabilities may receive services within their classroom from the center's therapist or school district itinerant teacher. Some children spend part of the day in nonintegrated or integrated special education classroom and return to City Center for the remainder of the day.

Program 4: Valley View

This is a preschool program housed within a public high school in a rural area. There are 16 children with disabilities in a class of 32 children. The families of children who are typically developing pay a monthly fee for the preschool and provide their own transportation. The children with disabilities are funded by state and federal sources, and transportation is provided by the school district. Families are primarily Caucasian and middle to upper class.

The program is located in the southern part of the state. A special education teacher leads the class in collaboration with a family studies teacher. The special education teacher develops and implements the IEPs with input from families and related service professionals. Children with disabilities receive direct services from speech/language therapists and occupational therapists within the classroom on a regular weekly schedule. High school students participate in the preschool by serving as tutors. Each student is assigned a child and interacts with that child, with guidance and assistance from the preschool teachers.

About the Editor and the Contributors

Paula J. Beckman is Professor of Special Education at the University of Maryland. She is the author or co-author of numerous articles and books on early childhood special education. Recently, she was the co-author with Marci Hanson on a set of materials, entitled *Me Too!*, designed for family members who are interested in inclusive placements and community opportunities for their young children with disabilities. She coordinates a personnel preparation program for low-incidence disabilities and actively works with early childhood programs in other countries. Her research interests revolve around issues related to families and their children with disabilities.

William H. Brown is Associate Professor of Special Education in the Department of Educational Psychology and an affiliated faculty member with the Institute for Families in Society at the University of South Carolina at Columbia. Dr. Brown has been a teacher, a parent trainer, a service coordinator, a director of a large university-affiliated early intervention program, a consultant to early childhood and early childhood special education programs, an advocate for enhanced services for young children and adults with disabilities, and president of the Nashville/Davidson County and Tennessee Association for Retarded Citizens (ARC). His current professional interests focus on early intervention, prevention, young children's social competence, family support services for preschoolers and young children with and without disabilities, and personnel preparation of early childhood and early childhood special educators.

Marci J. Hanson is Professor at San Francisco State University, Department of Special Education. She coordinates early childhood special education and the SFSU Joint Doctoral Program in Special Education with UC Berkeley. Dr. Hanson is also a member of the Child and Adolescent Development faculty of the Marian Wright Edelman Institute for the Study of Children, Youth and Families at SFSU. Dr. Hanson has had extensive experience developing and implementing early intervention programs for disabled infants, toddlers, and preschoolers and their families and has focused on issues of cross-cultural competence in recent years. She has contributed actively to the peer-reviewed professional literature and she has authored, co-authored, and edited numerous books on early intervention.

Eva Horn is Associate Professor of Early Childhood Special Education at the University of Kansas. Dr. Horn's professional career has focused on the development of effective instructional approaches for infants and young children with developmental delays and disabilities. Her research has centered on how these effective strategies can be implemented within the context of ongoing routines and activities in inclusive environments. The translation of research to practice is central to her extensive work in personnel preparation and development. Dr. Horn is the new editor of the journal *Young Exceptional Children.*

Shouming Li served as the Research Coordinator for ECRII in the University of Maryland from 1994 to 1999. His research interests have been mixed-method research design and computer-assisted educational research. He received his Ph.D. from the State University of New York at Albany.

Joan Lieber is Professor of Special Education in the College of Education at the University of Maryland, where she teaches graduate and undergraduate courses and conducts research. Her research interests include inclusion and teachers' beliefs and practices. She has eight years of public school teaching experience in preschool inclusive classrooms and in elementary grades. She currently co-directs an early childhood special education model demonstration project that includes young children with disabilities in community-based programs.

Jules Marquart is Director of Policy, Planning and Research at the Tennessee Department of Children's Services. She has been involved in evaluation and research on employer-sponsored child care programs, the child care system in Singapore, children's mental health services, services integration initiatives, preschool inclusion programs, and child welfare programs.

Samuel L. Odom (Editor) is Otting Professor of Special Education at Indiana University. He previously held faculty positions in special education at the University of North Carolina at Chapel Hill and Peabody College of Vanderbilt University. He has authored many journal articles and book chapters about programs for young children and their families, and is the co-editor of four books on early childhood special education. In 1999, Dr. Odom received the Research in Special Education Award from the Special Education Research SIG of AERA, and he has served on the National Academy of Sciences Committee on Educational Interventions for Young Children with Autism. His research addresses issues related to the inclusion of typically developing children and young children with disabilities in early childhood education settings and intervention to promote the peer-related social competence of young children with autism.

Susan R. Sandall is Assistant Professor in the area of special education at the University of Washington with a specialization in early intervention/ early childhood special education. She has published materials on instructional strategies to facilitate optimal outcomes for young children with disabilities, directed personnel preparation projects, and developed curriculum materials for all age groups from infants to adults. She is a board member of the Division for Early Childhood (DEC), Council for Exceptional Children and an investigator on DEC's research project to synthesize and translate EI/ECSE research practice to recommended practices for the field. She is also the co-editor of DEC's new monograph series.

Ilene S. Schwartz is Professor in the area of special education at the University of Washington. Dr. Schwartz has an extensive background working with young children with special needs, specifically with young children with autism and other severe disabilities. She is the principal investigator of a model demonstration project to develop school-based services for young children with autism, a research project to assess the differential effectiveness of preschool programs for young children with autism, and a personnel preparation program to prepare early childhood teachers who work with children with severe disabilities in inclusive settings. Dr. Schwartz has published numerous book chapters and journal articles about early childhood special education and social validity.

Jennifer Tschantz is currently a doctoral student at the University of Maryland, College Park. Previously she was an early childhood special educator in Georgia, where she worked in several inclusive preschool settings. She received her master's degree in early childhood special education from the University of Georgia. Her research interests include examining the factors and policies impacting collaboration and the inclusion of children with disabilities in Head Start and Early Head Start.

Ruth A. Wolery is Assistant Professor of the Practice of Special Education at Peabody College of Vanderbilt University and Director of the Susan

Gray School for Children. Prior to joining the ECRII team, she spent many years working in the public school system. Her current teaching and research interests focus on delivering high-quality services to young children with disabilities in inclusive preschool programs.

Pamela J. Wolfberg is a founding director of the Autism Institute on Peer Relations and Play–Center for Integrated Play Groups in San Francisco. Her research and practice centers on efforts to develop inclusive peer play programs. She actively leads seminars for practitioners and families throughout the United States and abroad. She is widely published in academic texts, peer-reviewed journals, and books. Her newest book, *Play and Imagination in Children with Autism* (Teachers College Press, 1999), is based on her doctoral dissertation, for which she received a distinguished award from the University of California, Berkeley. She also serves on the editorial board of JASH and as an associate editor for *Autism: The International Journal of Research and Practice.*

Craig Zercher is currently a doctoral student in the Joint Doctoral Program in Special Education at UC Berkeley and San Francisco State University. He has served as the director of a therapeutic preschool program for young children with emotional and behavioral disorders and designed and directed preventive programs for children at risk for expulsion from Head Start and state child development centers. He is currently completing dissertation research examining the conflict behavior of preschool children with conduct problems.

Index